A DOCUMENTARY HISTORY BASED UPON AN EXHIBIT IN THE NATIONAL ARCHIVES BUILDING

The Formation of the Union

WASHINGTON, D. C.

List of Documents

ENGRAVED by W. I. STONE for the Dept. of State by order of J. Q. ADAMS Sec. of State July 4th 1823.

IN CONGRESS, JULY 4, 1776.

The unanimous Declaration of the thirteen united States of America,

When in the Course of human events it becomes necessary for one people to dissolve the political bands which have connected them with another, and to assume among the powers of the earth, the separate and equal station to which the Laws of Nature and of Nature's God entitle them, a decent respect to the opinions of mankind requires that they should declare the causes which impel them to the separation. —— We hold these truths to be self-evident, that all men are created equal, that they are endowed by their Creator with certain unalienable Rights, that among these are Life, Liberty and the pursuit of Happiness. — That to secure these rights, Governments are instituted among Men, deriving their just powers from the consent of the governed, — That whenever any Form of Government becomes destructive of these ends, it is the Right of the People to alter or to abolish it, and to institute new Government, laying its foundation on such principles and organizing its powers in such form, as to them shall seem most likely to effect their Safety and Happiness. Prudence, indeed, will dictate that Governments long established should not be changed for light and transient causes; and accordingly all experience hath shewn, that mankind are more disposed to suffer, while evils are sufferable, than to right themselves by abolishing the forms to which they are accustomed. But when a long train of abuses and usurpations, pursuing invariably the same Object evinces a design to reduce them under absolute Despotism, it is their right, it is their duty, to throw off such Government, and to provide new Guards for their future security. — Such has been the patient sufferance of these Colonies; and such is now the necessity which constrains them to alter their former Systems of Government. The history of the present King of Great Britain is a history of repeated injuries and usurpations, all having in direct object the establishment of an absolute Tyranny over these States. To prove this, let Facts be submitted to a candid world. —— He has refused his Assent to Laws, the most wholesome and necessary for the public good. —— He has forbidden his Governors to pass Laws of immediate and pressing importance, unless suspended in their operation till his Assent should be obtained; and when so suspended, he has utterly neglected to attend to them. —— He has refused to pass other Laws for the accommodation of large districts of people, unless those people would relinquish the right of Representation in the Legislature, a right inestimable to them and formidable to tyrants only. —— He has called together legislative bodies at places unusual, uncomfortable, and distant from the depository of their public Records, for the sole purpose of fatiguing them into compliance with his measures. —— He has dissolved Represtative Houses repeatedly, for opposing with manly firmness his invasions on the rights of the people. —— He has refused for a long time, after such dissolutions, to cause others to be elected; whereby the Legislative powers, incapable of Annihilation, have returned to the People at large for their exercise; the State remaining in the mean time exposed to all the dangers of invasion from without, and convulsions within. —— He has endeavoured to prevent the population of these States; for that purpose obstructing the Laws for Naturalization of Foreigners; refusing to pass others to encourage their migrations hither, and raising the conditions of new Appropriations of Lands. —— He has obstructed the Administration of Justice, by refusing his Assent to Laws for establishing Judiciary powers. —— He has made Judges dependent on his Will alone, for the tenure of their offices, and the amount and payment of their salaries. —— He has erected a multitude of New Offices, and sent hither swarms of Officers to harrass our people, and eat out their substance. —— He has kept among us, in times of peace, Standing Armies without the Consent of our legislatures. —— He has affected to render the Military independent of and superior to the Civil power. —— He has combined with others to subject us to a jurisdiction foreign to our constitution, and unacknowledged by our laws; giving his Assent to their Acts of pretended Legislation: — For Quartering large bodies of armed troops among us: — For protecting them, by a mock Trial, from punishment for any Murders which they should commit on the Inhabitants of these States: — For cutting off our Trade with all parts of the world: — For imposing Taxes on us without our Consent: — For depriving us in many cases, of the benefits of Trial by Jury: — For transporting us beyond Seas to be tried for pretended offences — For abolishing the free System of English Laws in a neighbouring Province, establishing therein an Arbitrary government, and enlarging its Boundaries so as to render it at once an example and fit instrument for introducing the same absolute rule into these Colonies: — For taking away our Charters, abolishing our most valuable Laws, and altering fundamentally the Forms of our Governments: — For suspending our own Legislatures, and declaring themselves invested with power to legislate for us in all cases whatsoever. — He has abdicated Government here, by declaring us out of his Protection and waging War against us. —— He has plundered our seas, ravaged our Coasts, burnt our towns, and destroyed the lives of our people. —— He is at this time transporting large Armies of foreign Mercenaries to compleat the works of death, desolation and tyranny, already begun with circumstances of Cruelty & perfidy scarcely paralleled in the most barbarous ages, and totally unworthy the Head of a civilized nation. —— He has constrained our fellow Citizens taken Captive on the high Seas to bear Arms against their Country, to become the executioners of their friends and Brethren, or to fall themselves by their Hands. —— He has excited domestic insurrections amongst us, and has endeavoured to bring on the inhabitants of our frontiers, the merciless Indian Savages, whose known rule of warfare, is an undistinguished destruction of all ages, sexes and conditions. In every stage of these Oppressions We have Petitioned for Redress in the most humble terms: Our repeated Petitions have been answered only by repeated injury. A Prince, whose character is thus marked by every act which may define a Tyrant, is unfit to be the ruler of a free people. Nor have We been wanting in attentions to our Brittish brethren. We have warned them from time to time of attempts by their legislature to extend an unwarrantable jurisdiction over us. We have reminded them of the circumstances of our emigration and settlement here. We have appealed to their native justice and magnanimity, and we have conjured them by the ties of our common kindred to disavow these usurpations, which, would inevitably interrupt our connections and correspondence. They too have been deaf to the voice of justice and of consanguinity. We must, therefore, acquiesce in the necessity, which denounces our Separation, and hold them, as we hold the rest of mankind, Enemies in War, in Peace Friends. ——

We, therefore, the Representatives of the united States of America, in General Congress, Assembled, appealing to the Supreme Judge of the world for the rectitude of our intentions, do, in the Name, and by Authority of the good People of these Colonies, solemnly publish and declare, That these United Colonies are, and of Right ought to be Free and Independent States; that they are Absolved from all Allegiance to the British Crown, and that all political connection between them and the State of Great Britain, is and ought to be totally dissolved; and that as Free and Independent States, they have full Power to levy War, conclude Peace, contract Alliances, establish Commerce, and to do all other Acts and Things which Independent States may of right do. —— And for the support of this Declaration, with a firm reliance on the protection of divine Providence, we mutually pledge to each other our Lives, our Fortunes and our sacred Honor.

John Hancock

Button Gwinnett
Lyman Hall
Geo Walton.

Wm Hooper
Joseph Hewes,
John Penn

Edward Rutledge 1.
Thos Heyward Junr.
Thomas Lynch Junr.
Arthur Middleton

Samuel Chase
Wm Paca
Thos Stone
Charles Carroll of Carrollton

George Wythe
Richard Henry Lee
Th Jefferson
Benj Harrison
Thos Nelson jr.
Francis Lightfoot Lee
Carter Braxton

Robt Morris
Benjamin Rush
Benja. Franklin
John Morton
Geo Clymer
Jas. Smith
Geo. Taylor
James Wilson
Geo. Ross
Caesar Rodney
Geo Read
Thos M:Kean

Wm Floyd
Phil. Livingston
Frans. Lewis
Lewis Morris
Richd Stockton
Jno Witherspoon
Fras. Hopkinson
John Hart
Abra Clark

Josiah Bartlett
Wm Whipple
Saml Adams
John Adams
Robt Treat Paine
Elbridge Gerry
Step. Hopkins
William Ellery
Roger Sherman
Sam el Huntington
Wm Williams
Oliver Wolcott
Matthew Thornton

THE DECLARATION OF INDEPENDENCE

The Formation of the Union

Between September 5, 1774, when the First Continental Congress met in Philadelphia, and December 15, 1791, when the Bill of Rights became part of the Constitution of the United States, the course of American history was set for centuries to come.

Thirteen small and separate Colonies—in many cases having little in common besides their fealty to Great Britain—declared themselves independent states, secured recognition from foreign powers and made an alliance with France, defeated Great Britain on the field of battle, and negotiated a treaty of peace with favorable territorial provisions. Experimenting and innovating as they went, the new States established a completely original non-colonial policy for territorial acquisitions. When a confederation—their earliest form of government—appeared inadequate, they changed their political structure, in peaceful revolution, to a federal union under man's first written national constitution with specific guarantees of individual freedom in the Bill of Rights.

The Americans who travelled this remarkable route were wise in the ways of politics after their long experience of virtual self-government within the British Empire and could boast a high level of literacy for the period in which they lived. The canny lawyers and businessmen they chose to lead the American Revolution were careful to leave a written record of most of the steps in the formation of the American Union.

"...these united colonies...ought to be free..."

The Grievances

Most American colonial subjects of the King of England were reasonably content with the position of the American Colonies in the British Empire before the end of the French and Indian War in 1763. Nearly all of the Colonies enjoyed near-autonomy under a governor appointed by the Crown, and they elected assemblies which made most local laws; the Navigation Acts which confined much colonial trade to British ports and British ships were not onerous and assured American merchants of a steady market. The advantages of belonging to the British Empire outweighed the disadvantages until the British Parliament decided to tax the colonists to pay for their recent defense against the French and Indians and for their future administration.

Several taxes, including the Stamp Act and the Townshend Acts, were levied, then repealed when Americans protested that only their own legislatures could tax them. Finally, however, the granting of a monopoly of the colonial tea market to the British East India Company brought matters to a head. When Bostonians staged the Boston Tea Party, staining the waters of their harbor with East India tea, Parliament retaliated with a series of laws called the Cœrcive Acts in England, but promptly labeled the "Intolerable Acts" in America. Among other things, the Acts closed the port of Boston and severely limited popular government in Massachusetts, striking at what Americans considered their right to make their own laws. Fearing that the same treatment awaited any other colony which displeased Parliament, all the Colonies except Georgia sent delegates to Philadelphia to formulate a united stand on British colonial policy.

The First Continental Congress

Few of the delegates to the First Continental Congress were considering independence from Great Britain as they took their seats in Carpenters' Hall in Philadelphia on the 5th of September 1774. Even though Massachusetts had sent such radical leaders as Samuel Adams and his cousin John Adams, the credentials of the Massachusetts delegates declared that the Congress was to "consult upon the present state of the Colonies, . . . and determine upon wise and proper measures, to be by them recommended to all the Colonies, for the recovery of their just rights & liberties, civil and religious, and the restoration of union and harmony between Great Britain and the Colonies. . . ."

Virtually the first order of business was a unanimous resolution on September 6 to appoint a committee "to state the rights of the Colonies . . . and the means most proper to be pursued for obtaining the restoration of them." Two delegates from each colony made up the committee. Both Adamses were on it, along with Roger Sherman of Connecticut, John Jay of New York, and Richard Henry Lee and Edmund Pendleton of Virginia.

The Declaration of Rights (document 1), passed October 14, 1774, carried out the mandate to "state the rights of the Colonies." Following a long preamble detailing the grievances which had led to the meeting of the Continental Congress, there were 10 resolutions. Americans, they declared, were

The good people of the several colonies of Newhampshire, Massachusetts-bay, Rhode island and Providence plantations, Connecticut, Newyork, New-Jersey, Pensylvania, New castle Kent and Sussex on Delaware, Maryland, Virginia, North Carolina and South Carolina justly alarmed at these arbitrary proceedings of parliament and administration have severally elected, consti= tuted and appointed deputies to meet and sit in general congress in the city of Philadelphia in order to obtain such establishment as that their religion, laws and liberties may not be subverted:

Whereupon the deputies so appointed being now assembled in a full and free representation of these colonies, taking into their most serious consideration, the best means of attaining the ends aforesaid do in the first place as Englishmen their ancestors in like cases have usually done, for asserting and vindicating their rights and liberties Declare

That the inhabitants of the English colonies in North America by the immutable laws of Nature, the principles of the English constitution, and the several charters or compacts have the following Rights.

1. Resolved N.C.D. 1. That they are entitled to life, liberty & property: and they have never ceded to any sovereign power whatever a right to dispose of either without their consent.

Resolved N.C.D. 2. That our ancestors, who first settled these colonies were, at the time of their emigration from the mother country, entitled to all the rights, liberties and immunities of free and natural born subjects, within the realm of England.

Resolved

1. *THE DECLARATION OF RIGHTS, October 14, 1774, PCC No. 1, Rough Journal of Congress, I: 44-46, RG 360, Records of the Continental and Confederation Congresses and the Constitutional Convention. 12 x 7⅜ in. 3 pages (pages 44 and 45 illustrated).*

Resolved N.C.D. 3. That by such emigration, they by no means forfeited, surrendered or lost any of those rights, but that they were, and their descendants now are entitled to the exercise and enjoyment of all such of them, as their local and other circumstances enable them to exercise and enjoy.

Resolved. 4. That the foundation of english liberty and of all free government is a right in the people, to participate in their legislative council: and as the english colonists are not represented, and from their local and other circum=stances cannot be properly represented in the British parliament, they are entitled to a free and exclusive power of legislation in their several provincial legislatures, where their right of representation can alone be preserved, in all cases of taxation and internal polity, subject only to the negative of their sovereign, in such manner, as has been heretofore used and accustomed: But, from the necessity of the case, and a regard to the mutual interests of both countries, we cheerfully consent to the operation of such acts of the British parliament, as are bona fide, restrained to the regulation of our external commerce, for the purpose of securing the commercial advantages of the whole empire to the mother country, and the commercial benefits of its respective members, excluding every idea of taxation internal or external for raising a revenue on the subjects in America without their consent.

Resolved N.C.D. 5. That the respective colonies are entitled to the common law of England, and more especially to the great and inestimable priviledge of being tried by their peers of the vicinage according to the course of that law.

Resolved.

entitled to the same "rights, liberties, and immunities of free and natural-born subjects, within the realm of England" which their ancestors had enjoyed before emigrating to the colonies.

Resolution 4 presented the crux of the problem:

> That the foundation of english liberty, and of all free government is a right in the people, to participate in their legislative council: and as the English colonists are not represented, and from their local and other circumstances cannot properly be represented in the British parliament, they are entitled to a free and exclusive power of legislation in their several provincial legislatures, where their right of representation can alone be preserved, in all cases of taxation and internal polity, subject only to the negative of their sovereign, in such manner as has been heretofore used and accustomed: But, from the necessity of the case, and a regard to the mutual interests of both countries, we cheerfully consent to the operation of such acts of the British parliament, as are bona fide, restrained to the regulation of our external commerce, for the purpose of securing the commercial advantages of the whole empire to the mother country, and the commercial benefits of its respective members excluding every idea of taxation internal or external for raising a revenue on the subjects in America without their consent.

The right of the colonists "peaceably to assemble, consider of their grievances, and petition the King" was also asserted, and the ninth resolution declared that "the keeping of a Standing army in these colonies, in times of peace, without the consent of the legislature of that colony, in which such army is kept, is against the law."

The Articles of Association (document 2), a nonimportation, nonconsumption, nonexportation agreement, was agreed upon on October 20 as "the means most proper . . . for obtaining restoration" of these rights. Effective December 1, 1774, no goods from Great Britain or Ireland were to be imported, and the slave trade was to be discontinued. Three months later, nonconsumption of British goods would begin, and, if the offending Intolerable Acts had not been repealed by September 10, 1775, nonexportation was to be instituted: all American merchants would thereafter refuse to sell American goods to the mother country.

The preamble of the Articles read in part:

> We, his Majesty's most loyal subjects . . . affected with the deepest anxiety and most alarming apprehensions at those grievances and distresses, with which his Majesty's American subjects are oppressed, and having taken under our most serious deliberation the state of the whole continent find, that the present unhappy situation of our affairs is occasioned by a ruinous System of colony administration adopted by the British Ministry . . . evidently calculated for enslaving these colonies and with them the British Empire.

Then, after listing acts of Parliament to which the colonists objected, the preamble concluded:

> To obtain redress of these grievances, which threaten destruction to the lives, liberty and property of his Majesty's subjects in North-America we are of opinion, that a non-importation, non-consumption and non-exportation agreem[ent] faithfully adhered to will prove the most speedy, effectual and peaceable measure: And therefore we do for ourselves and the inhabitants of the several colonies whom we represent firmly agree and associate under the sacred ties of virtue, honour and love of our country as follows.

After the preamble were listed 14 articles, including several that called for a condemnation of colonial merchants, shipowners, and others who should disregard the Articles, and for nonintercourse with any colony or province that should refuse to accede to or should violate the Articles of Association.

Several of the articles were designed to offset the economic dislocations that Congress realized were likely to occur. One article prohibited the sale of goods at rates higher than those that had prevailed "for twelve months last past"; another stated that

> . . . we will in our several stations encourage frugality, œconomy and industry and promote agriculture, arts and manufactures of this country, especially that of wool, and will discountenance and discourage every species of extravagance and dissipation especially all horse racing and all kinds of gaming, cockfighting, exhibitions of plays, shews and other expensive diversions and entertainments. . . .

Other important provisions were that the committees of correspondence should inspect customhouse records and that every county, city, and town should elect a committee to observe "the conduct of all persons touching this association" and to publish the names of violators as "enemies of American liberty."

Committees of observation and inspection, promptly set up, did much to enforce the Articles. Even more important, they formed a well organized and powerful network which, after Lexington and Concord, was used to promote military as well as economic union.

The Association was adopted with great optimism regarding its effectiveness and was expected to bring Great Britain to terms in short order. Nonimportation agreements among merchants of individual colonies were credited with having forced Parliament to repeal both the Stamp Act and the Townshend Acts in the years between 1765 and 1770. Surely a boycott embracing 12 of the Thirteen Colonies would be even more successful.

When these two important documents had been signed, the First Continental Congress finished its other business quickly. It dispatched a petition to the King and sent addresses to the people of Great Britain, of North America, and of Quebec, stating the colonial position and soliciting support.

"The Congress then dissolved itself" on October

1.

343

We, his Majesty's most loyal subjects the Delegates of the several Colonies of New Hampshire, Massachusetts-Bay, Rhode Island, Connecticut, New York, New Jersey, Pennsylvania, The three lower counties of Newcastle, Kent and Sussex on Delaware, Maryland, Virginia, North Carolina and South Carolina deputed to represent them in a continental Congress held in the city of Philadelphia on the fifth day of September 1774. avowing our allegiance to his Majesty, our affection and regard for our fellow subjects in Great-Britain and elsewhere affected with the deepest anxiety and most alarming apprehensions at those grievances and distresses, with which his Majesty's American subjects are oppressed, and having taken under our most serious deliberation the state of the whole continent find, that the present unhappy situation of our affairs is occasioned by a ruinous system of colony administration adopted by the British Ministry about the year 1763 evidently calculated for enslaving these colonies and with them the British Empire. In prosecution of which system various acts of parliament have been passed for raising a Revenue in America, for depriving the American subjects in many instances of the constitutional trial by jury, exposing their lives to danger by directing a new and illegal trial beyond the seas for crimes alleged to have been committed in America: And in prosecution of the same system, several late cruel and oppressive acts have been passed respecting the town of Boston and the Massachusetts-Bay, and also an act for extending the province of Quebec so as to border on the western frontiers of these colonies, establishing an arbitrary government therein and discouraging the settlement of British subjects in that wide extended country, thus by the influence of civil principles and ancient prejudices to dispose the inhabitants to act with hostility against the free protestant colonies, whenever a wicked Ministry shall chuse so to direct them. —

To obtain redress of these grievances, which threaten destruction to the lives, liberty and property of his Majesty's subjects in North-America we are of opinion, that a non-importation, non-consumption and non-exportation agreement faithfully adhered to will prove the most speedy, effectual and peaceable measure: And therefore we do for ourselves and the inhabitants of the several colonies whom we represent firmly agree and associate under the sacred ties of virtue, honour and love of our country as follows.

1. That from and after the first day of December next we will not import into British America from Great-Britain or Ireland, any Goods, wares or merchandize whatsoever or from any other place any such goods, wares or merchandize as shall have been exported from Great-Britain or Ireland; nor will we after that day import any East India Tea from any part of the World, nor any Molasses, Syrups, paneles, Coffee or Piemento from the British Plantations or from Dominica, nor Wines from Madeira or the Western Islands nor foreign Indigo. —

2. That we will neither import nor purchase any Slave imported after the first day of December next, and after which time we will wholly discontinue the Slave trade, and will neither be concerned in it ourselves, nor will we hire our vessels nor sell our commodities or manufactures to those who are concerned in it. —

3. As a non-consumption agreement strictly adhered to will be an effectual security for the observation of the non-importation we as above solemnly agree and associate, that from this day we will not purchase or use any Tea imported on account of the East India Company, or any on which a duty hath been or shall be paid; and from and after the first day of March next, we will not purchase or use any East India tea whatever, nor will we nor shall any person for or under us purchase or use any of those goods, wares or merchandize we have agreed not to import, which we shall know or have cause to suspect were imported after the first day of December except such as come under the rules and directions of the tenth article hereafter mentioned.

4. The earnest desire we have not to injure our fellow subjects in Great-Britain, Ireland or the West-Indies induces us to suspend a non-exportation until the tenth day of September 1775. At which time if the said acts and parts of acts of the British Parliament herein after mentioned are not repealed we will not directly or indirectly export any merchandize or commodity whatsoever to Great-Britain, Ireland or the West-Indies, except Rice to Europe.

5. Such as are merchants and use the British and Irish trade will give orders as soon as possible to their factors, Agents and Correspondents in Great-Britain and Ireland not to ship any goods to them on any pretence whatsoever as they cannot be received in America; And if any merchant residing in Great-Britain or Ireland shall directly or indirectly ship any goods, wares or merchandize for America in order to break the said non-importation agreement or in any manner contravene the

2. *THE ARTICLES OF ASSOCIATION, October 20, 1774, Miscellaneous Papers of the Continental Congress, RG 360. 18¼ x 14¾ in. Signed by delegates of 12 colonies. 3 pages (pages 1 and 3 illustrated).*

foreign paper, glass and painters colours imported into America, and extend the powers of the admiralty courts beyond their ancient limits, deprive the American subject of trial by jury, authorize the judges certificate to indemnify the prosecutor from damages, that he might otherwise be liable to from a trial by his peers, require oppressive security from a claimant of ships or goods seized, before he shall be allowed to defend his property, are repealed.— And until that part of the Act of the 12 G. 3. ch. 24 entitled an Act for the better securing his Majesty's dock yards, magazines, ships ammunition and stores" by which any person charged with committing any of the offences therein described, in America, may be tried in any shire or county within the realm is repealed. And until the four acts passed in the last session of Parliament viz. that for stopping the port and blocking up the harbour of Boston— that for altering the charter and government of the Massachusetts Bay— and that which is entitled an act for the better administration of Justice &c, and that for extending the limits of Quebec &c are repealed. And we recommend it to the provincial conventions and to the committees in the respective colonies to establish such farther regulations as they may think proper for carrying into execution this association.—

The foregoing association being determined upon by the Congress, was ordered to be subscribed by the several Members thereof and thereupon we have hereunto set our respective names accordingly.

In Congress, Philadelphia October 20th. 1774.—

Peyton Randolph President

[N]ew Hamp[shi]re — Jno. Sullivan, Nathl. Folsom

[M]assachusetts [Ba]y — Thomas Cushing, Saml. Adams, John Adams, Robt. Treat Paine

[Rhode Island] — Step. Hopkins, Sam: Ward

Connecticut — Eliphalet Dyer, Roger Sherman, Silas Deane

[N]ew York — Isaac Low, John Alsop, John Jay, Jas. Duane, Phil. Livingston, Wm. Floyd, Henry Wisner, S. Boerum

[N]ew Jersey — J. Kinsey, Wil: Livingston, Stepn. Crane, Richd. Smith, John De Hart

Pennsylvania — Jos. Galloway, John Dickinson, Chas. Humphreys, Thomas Mifflin, E. Biddle, John Morton, Geo: Ross

The Lower Counties New Castle &c. — Cæsar Rodney, Tho. M:Kean, Geo: Read

Maryland — Mat. Tilghman, Ths. Johnson Junr., Wm. Paca, Samuel Chase

Virginia — Richard Henry Lee, G. Washington, P. Henry Jr., Richard Bland, Benj. Harrison, Edmd. Pendleton

North Carolina — Will Hooper, Joseph Hewes, R. Caswell

South Carolina — Henry Middleton, Thos. Lynch, Christ. Gadsden, J. Rutledge, Edward Rutledge

(Continuation of Document 2)

26, but a resolution had been passed providing for the meeting of a Second Continental Congress on May 10, 1775, "unless the redress of grievances, which we have desired, be obtained before that time." Thus the First Continental Congress served notice that it did not consider itself an isolated protest meeting, but represented the beginning of a determined defense of American freedom.

Without conscious intention, the leaders of the American colonies had taken the first important step toward becoming the United States of America.

The Revolutionary War: First Shots

While the First Continental Congress was seeking the peaceful restoration of the rights of the colonies within the British Empire, the farmers of Massachusetts were preparing for war. Companies of "minutemen" were secretly drilling, and arms and ammunition were being collected and hidden in anticipation of armed clashes with the British.

At the end of the French and Indian War, a standing army of British soldiers had been left in America for the first time in peacetime. In 1774, General Thomas Gage, the British Commander in Chief, was given the additional position of Royal Governor of Massachusetts and charged with the unpleasant duty of enforcing the punitive Intolerable Acts. Urged by the British Ministry to act against the unrepentant colonists by seizing the leaders, Gage reluctantly decided to send troops to arrest Samuel Adams and John Hancock, who had fled to Lexington, and to proceed to Concord to capture military stores known to be hidden there.

On the evening of April 18, 1775, General Gage's "secret" expedition of about 800 troops left Boston for Lexington and Concord. His plans were quickly discovered, and William Dawes and Paul Revere slipped out of the city on their famous rides to warn Adams, Hancock, and the people of the two towns.

When the British arrived at Lexington early on the morning of April 19, a little band of minutemen under the command of Captain John Parker was drawn up on the village green to greet them. Parker's deposition describes his version of what happened thereafter:

> I John Parker, of lawful Age, and Commander of the Militia in Lexington, do testify & declare that on the 19th Instant, in the Morning, about one of the Clock, being informed that there were a Number of Regular Officers riding up and down the Road, stopping and insulting People as they passed the Road, and also was informed that a Number of Regular Troops were on their March from Boston, in order to take the Province Stores at Concord, ordered our Militia to meet on the Common in said Lexington, to consult what to do, and concluded not to be discovered, nor meddle or make with said Regular Troops (if they should approach) unless they should insult or molest us—and upon their sudden Approach I immediately ordered our Militia to disperse and not to fire—Immediately said Troops made their Appearance and rushed furiously, fired upon and killed eight of our Party, without receiving any Provocation therefor from us. (Document 3.)

Following this skirmish, the British soldiers moved on to Concord where they found few military supplies to seize because the forewarned Americans had removed them to other hiding places. The entire day's expedition was costly to the British as they encountered one American militia unit after another, and made their way back to Boston under steady sniping. The Americans fought Indian style, firing on the British from behind trees and stone walls. At the same time, the Massachusetts Provincial Congress, a revolutionary body elected after the Royal Governor had dissolved the colonial legislature, realized that war had come at last. Fully aware that Massachusetts could not undertake to fight the British alone, it prepared an appeal for assistance (document 4) to be sent to the Continental Congress, enclosing Parker's deposition and 19 others. It called upon the Congress to establish an American Army to fight in "the cause of America."

Meanwhile, on May 10, 1775, the very day that the Second Continental Congress began its deliberations, Ethan Allen and his Green Mountain Boys, on their own initiative, surprised the British garrison at Fort Ticonderoga. By his own account Allen secured the surrender in the name of "the great Jehovah and the Continental Congress." Whether or not his recollection was accurate, the Second Continental Congress could no longer hope for an entirely peaceful settlement of colonial differences with England.

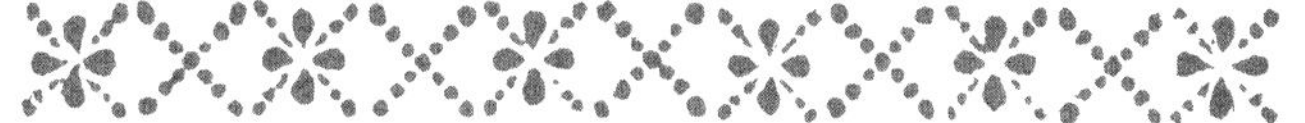

No. 4. Lexington April 25th, 1775. [5]

I John Parker, of lawfull Age, and Commander of the Militia in Lexington, do testify & declare that on the 19th Instant, in the Morning, about one of the Clock, being informed that there were a Number of Regular Officers riding up and down the Road, stopping and insulting People as they passed the Road, and also was informed that a Number of Regular Troops were on their March from Boston, in order to take the Province Stores at Concord, ordered our Militia to meet on the Common in said Lexington, to consult what to do, and concluded not to be discovered, nor meddle or make with said Regular Troops (if they should approach) unless they should insult or molest us — and upon their sudden Approach I immediately ordered our Militia to disperse and not to fire — Immediately said Troops made their Appearance and rushed furiously, fired upon and killed eight of our Party, without receiving any Provocation therefor from us.

John Parker

3. *THE BATTLE OF LEXINGTON: DEPOSITION BY CAPTAIN PARKER,* April 25, 1775. *PCC No. 65, Massachusetts State Papers, 1775-87, I: 17, RG 360. 11⅞ x 7¼ in. 1 page.*

The Second Continental Congress

The Second Continental Congress was, to all intents and purposes, the government of the United States from 1775 to 1788. Although its membership changed through the years, and it moved its meeting place from city to city during the Revolutionary War and until 1785, it was essentially the same body which declared the United States independent, waged the war to make independence a fact, and, as "the United States in Congress Assembled," regularized its own activities as the national government by writing the Articles of Confederation. It finally dissolved itself when a new Constitution replaced the Articles in 1788.

Many members of the First Continental Congress reappeared in the Second, but several new delegates presented credentials. Notable among them was Benjamin Franklin of Pennsylvania, who had

In Provincial Congress, Watertown, May 3d 1775.

To the Honorable American Continental Congress, to be conven'd at Philadelphia on the tenth of May Instant.—

May it please your Honours,

The Congress of this Colony, impressed with the deepest Concern for their Country under the present critical and alarming State of its public Affairs, beg leave with the most respectful Submission, whilst acting in Support of the Cause of America to request the direction & assistance of your respectable Assembly—

The inclosed Packet, containing the Copies of Depositions which we have dispatched for London, also an Address to the Inhabitants of Great Britain, and a Letter to our Colony Agent Benjamin Franklin Esq.r, are humbly submitted to your Consideration—

The sanguinary Zeal of the ministerial Army to ruin and destroy the Inhabitants of this Colony, in the Opinion of this Congress, hath rendered the Establishment of an [illegible] Army indispensably necessary— We have accordingly passed an unanimous Resolve for thirteen thousand six hundred Men to be forthwith

raised

4\. *APPEAL FOR ASSISTANCE FROM MASSACHUSETTS, May 3, 1775, PCC No. 65, I: 1-3, RG 360. 9¼ x 7⅜ in. Signed by Joseph Warren, temporary President of the Provincial Congress of Massachusetts Bay Colony. 3 pages (page 1 illustrated).*
Addressed: To/The Hon^a the President of the American/Continental Congress/in/Philadelphia. Endorsed: N° 1./Letter from the Congress of/Massachusetts bay to the conti-/nental Congress. dated Watertown/May 3. 1775/rec^d & read May 11th

In Assembly

May 6.th 1775 A.M.

Resolved N. C. D.

That Benjamin Franklin Esqr. be, and he is hereby added to the Deputies appointed by this House to attend the Continental Congress expected to meet the 10.th Instant in this City

Resolved N. C. D.

That the Hon.ble Thomas Willing of Philadelphia, and James Wilson Esqr. of Carlisle be also added to the said Deputies for this Province

Extract from the Journals
Cha.s Moore, Clk
of Assembly

5. CREDENTIALS OF PENNSYLVANIA DELEGATES TO THE SECOND CONTINENTAL CONGRESS, May 6, 1775, Misc. PCC, RG 360.
9¼ x 7½ in. 1 page. The credentials of other Pennsylvania delegates besides Franklin, Willing and Wilson mentioned in the endorsement are separate documents. Endorsed: Credentials of/Edward Biddle/John Dickinson/Thomas Mifflin/Cha Humphreys/John Morton/George Ross/Benj Franklin/Thomas Willing/James Wilson/Delegates for/Pennsylvania/Read before the Congress May 11, 1775.

recently returned from London (document 5).

Gradually, almost imperceptibly, the Second Continental Congress took upon itself the responsibilities of a national government. The first dramatic decision, made only after days of debate, was the creation of a Continental Army. On June 14 a uniform method of enlistment was prescribed for companies to be raised in Pennsylvania, Maryland, and Virginia: "I ______________ have, this day, voluntarily enlisted myself, as a soldier, in the American continental army. . . ." The next day the shrewd New Englander John Adams engineered the nomination and unanimous election of a Virginian, Colonel George Washington, as the general

The President informed Col.o Washington that the Congress had yesterday, Unanimously made choice of him to be General & Commander in Chief of the American Forces, and requested he would accept of that Appointment; whereupon Col.o Washington, standing in his place, Spake as follows.

" Mr. President,

"Tho' I am truly sensible of the high Honour done me in this Appointment, yet I feel great distress, from a consciousness that my abilities & Military experience may not be equal to the extensive & important Trust: However, as the Congress desire I will enter upon the momentous duty, & exert every power I Possess In their service & for the support of the glorious Cause: I beg they will accept my most cordial thanks for this distinguished testimony of their Approbation.

But least some unlucky event should happen unfavourable to my reputation, I beg it may be remembered by every Gent.n in the room, that I this day declare with the utmost sincerity, I do not think my self equal to the Command I am honoured with.

As to pay, Sir, I beg leave to Assure the Congress that as no pecuniary consideration could have tempted me to have accepted this Arduous employment at ye expence of my domest. ease & happiness I do not wish to make any proffit from it: I will keep an exact Account of my expences; those I doubt not they will discharge & that is all I desire."

6. *WASHINGTON'S ACCEPTANCE OF THE POST OF COMMANDER IN CHIEF, June 16, 1775, PCC No. 152, Letters from Gen. George Washington, Commander in Chief of the Army, 1775-84, I: 1, RG 360. 11¾ x 7¾ in. 1 page. In the hand of Edmund Pendleton, a delegate from Virginia, except for the phrase "at ye expence of my domest ease & hap," which was interlined by Washington. Endorsed: Gen. Washington's answer/to the Congress upon his/Accepting the office*

who should "command all the continental forces, raised, or to be raised, for the defence of American liberty."

Washington was officially informed of his election on June 16 by Peyton Randolph of Virginia, president of the Congress.

> Whereupon Col^{o} Washington, standing in his place, Spoke as follows.
>
> "Mr President,
>
> "Tho' I am truly sensible of the high Honour done me in this Appointment, yet I feel great distress, from a consciousness that my abilities and military experience may not be equal to the extensive & important Trust: . . . .
>
> "But lest some unlucky event should happen unfavourable to my reputation, I beg it may be remembered by every Gent^{n} in the room, that I this day declare with the utmost sincerity, I do not think my self equal to the Command I [am] honoured with.
>
> As to pay, Sir, I beg leave to Assure the Congress that as no pecuniary consideration could have tempted me to have accepted this Arduous emploiment at ye expence of my domes^{t} ease & hap[iness] I do not wish to make any proffit from it: I will keep an exact Account of my expences; those I doubt not they will discharge & that is all I desire." (Document 6.)

Ten days later a Continental currency was established, and before the end of July a Post Office for the "United Colonies" was set up with headquarters in Philadelphia. Benjamin Franklin was unanimously chosen to be the first "postmaster General."

British Response to American Petitions

When the Second Continental Congress began its deliberations, King George III had made no official reply to the petition for redress of grievances sent to him by the First Continental Congress. Parliament had sent to the colonial legislature an offer of conciliation with no real expectation that its terms would be accepted, and they were not.

The determination of the King and Parliament to take a hard line with the colonies became increasingly evident as news of proclamations and acts came across the Atlantic. In August 1775, the King issued a proclamation declaring that his American subjects were "engaged in open and avowed rebellion," and he opened Parliament in October with a speech asserting that "the rebellious war now levied is become more general, and is manifestly carried on for the purpose of establishing an independent empire." Some Americans, like Samuel Adams, retorted that if the King thought they were fighting for independence, they might as well do so, but the majority of the Continental Congress still clung to the hope of reconciliation.

This hope dimmed when Parliament passed the American Prohibitory Act, described even by some members of Parliament as a "declaration of war" on America. It made all American vessels and their cargoes forfeit to the Crown "as if the same were the ships and effects of open enemies."

Finally, word reached the colonies that the King had negotiated treaties with German states to hire mercenaries to fight in America. George Washington secured copies of some of these agreements and sent them to Congress on May 23, 1776. Curiously, this action of the King—the hiring of Hessians—was what finally convinced many Americans that the mother country was indeed treating her colonies as a foreign country.

Reluctant Steps Toward Independence

Still the Continental Congress did not rush headlong into independence. One at a time, the ties with the mother country were cut, and it was only after separation from England was virtually a fact that a declaration of independence was issued.

The Privateering Resolution that "inhabitants of these colonies be permitted to fit out armed vessels to cruize [sic] on the enemies of these United Colonies," was an early indication that the United Colonies were becoming a sovereign state or group of states. Passed in March 1776, it also established rules and regulations to govern prize cases expected to arise from the capture of "enemy" vessels (document 7).

Two weeks later, on April 6, the ports of America were opened to the commerce of the world

Resolved That the inhabitants of these colonies be permitted to fit out armed vessels to cruise on the enemies of these united colonies.

7. *PRIVATEERING RESOLUTION, March 23, 1776, PCC No. 2, Transcript Journal of Congress, III: 382-383, RG 360. 12½ x 7¾ in. 2 pages (excerpt illustrated).*

(document 8). Since the Association and the Prohibitory Act effectively prevented trade with Great Britain, commerce with other nations was an economic necessity. Nevertheless, this was a de facto declaration of economic independence, severing the closest ties of the British Empire, the Navigation Acts which had bound the colonies to the mother country in one closed market.

Meanwhile, individual colonies were applying to the Continental Congress for advice on setting up local governments as royal governors first dissolved legislatures and then, in many cases, fled the colonies. On May 10, the Congress resolved

> That it be recommended to the respective assemblies and conventions of the united colonies, where no government sufficient to the exigences of their affairs have been hitherto established, to adopt such government as shall in the opinion of the representatives of the people best conduce to the happiness and safety of their constituents in particular and America in general. (Document 9A.)

The bitter tone of the preamble adopted 5 days later to be published with this resolution showed

Resolved That any goods wares and merchandize except staves and empty casks other than shaken or knocked down casks for molasses may be exported from the thirteen united colonies by the inhabitants thereof and by the people of all such countries as are not subject to the King of Great Britain to any parts of the world, which are not under the dominion of the said King:

Resolved That any goods wares & merchandize, except such as are of the growth, production or manufacture of or brought from any country under the dominion of the King of great Britain and except East India Tea may be imported from any other parts of the world to the thirteen United colonies by the inhabitants thereof and by the people of all such countries as are not subject to the said King,

8. *RESOLUTION OPENING AMERICAN PORTS TO WORLD COMMERCE, April 6, 1776, PCC No. 1, II: 58-59, RG 360. 12½ x 7¾ in. 2 pages (page 58 illustrated).*

that the patience of even the most conservative and loyal members of the Congress was nearing an end.

> Whereas his Britannic Majesty in conjunction with the lords and commons of great Britain has by a late act of Parliament excluded the inhabitants of these united colonies from the protection of his crown And whereas no answer whatever to the humble petitions of the colonies for redress of grievances & reconciliation with great Britain has been or is likely to be given; but the whole force of that Kingdom aided by foreign mercenaries is to be exerted for the destruction of the good people of these colonies, And whereas it appears absolutely irreconsileable to reason and good Conscience for the people of these colonies now to take the oaths and affirmations necessary for the support of any government under the crown of great Britain, and it is necessary that the exercise of every kind of authority under the said crown should be totally suppressed and all the powers of government exerted under the authority of the people of the colonies for the preservation of internal peace, virtue & good order as well as for the defence of their lives liberties and properties against the hostile invasions & cruel depredations of their enemies, therefore resolved &c. (Doc. 9B)

Little was now left of the structure of England's colonial empire on the American mainland between Quebec and Florida. The Thirteen Colonies were separated economically and politically from the mother country.

At the same time, the people were slowly becoming accustomed to the inevitability of independence as it began to be debated openly in the active colonial press. A pamphlet entitled *Common Sense*, written by Thomas Paine, denounced monarchy as "ridiculous" and called for independence because "there is something absurd, in supposing a Continent to be perpetually governed by an island." Within months of its publication in January 1776, thousands of copies had been sold, helping to convince its readers that "the cause of America is the cause of mankind."

In April North Carolina instructed its Continental Congress delegates to "concur with the delegates of the other colonies in declaring independency," and on May 4 Rhode Island declared itself independent.

The British burning of Norfolk and a Tory uprising in North Carolina helped to crystallize colonial thought. The drive toward freedom rapidly gained momentum; by the middle of May eight colonies had decided that they would join in supporting independence. The Convention of Virginia took a significant step on May 15 by passing the following resolution:

> Forasmuch as all the endeavours of the United Colonies by the most decent representations and petitions to the king and parliament of Great Britain to restore peace and security to America under the British government and a re-union with that people upon just and liberal terms instead of a redress of grievances have produced from an imperious and vindictive administration increased insult oppression and a vigorous attempt to effect our total destructions . . . .
>
> Resolved unanimously, that the delegates appointed to represent this colony in General Congress be instructed to propose to that respectable body to declare the United Colonies free and independent states, absolved from all allegiance to, or dependence upon, the crown or parliament of Great Britain; and that they give the assent of this colony to such declaration . . . . (Document 10.)

Resolved That it be recommended to the respective assemblies and conventions of the united colonies, where no government sufficient to the exigencies of their affairs have been hitherto established, to adopt such government as shall in the opinion of the representatives of the people best conduce to the happiness and safety of their constituents in particular and America in general.
Resolved That a committee of three be appointed to prepare a preamble to the foregoing resolution

9A. *RESOLUTION FOR THE FORMATION OF LOCAL GOVERNMENTS, May 10, 1776, PCC No. 2, III: 494, RG 360. 12 x 7¾ in. 1 page. (excerpt illustrated).*

follows

Whereas his Britannic Majesty in conjunction with the lords and commons of great Britain has by a late act of Parliament excluded the inhabitants of these united colonies from the protection of his crown — And whereas no answer whatever to the humble petitions of the colonies for redress of grievances & reconciliation with great Britain has been or is likely to be given; but the whole force of that kingdom aided by foreign mercenaries is to be exerted for the destruction of the good people of these colonies, And whereas it appears absolutely irreconcileable to reason and good Conscience for the people of these colonies now to take the oaths and affirmations necessary for the support of any government under the crown of great Britain, and it is necessary that the exercise of every kind of authority under the said crown should be totally suppressed and all the powers of government exerted under the authority of the people of the colonies for the preservation of internal peace, virtue & good order as well as for the defence of ~~our~~ their lives liberties and properties against the hostile invasions & cruel depredations of ~~our~~ their enemies, therefore resolved &c

Ordered that the ~~d~~ preamble with the resolution passed the 10th instant be published ...

9B. *PREAMBLE TO LOCAL GOVERNMENT RESOLUTION*, May 15, 1776, PCC No. 1, II: 149, RG 360. 12½ x 7¾ in. 1 page.

Resolved unanimously, that the delegates appointed to represent this colony in General Congress be instructed to propose to that respectable body to declare the United Colonies free and independent states, absolved from all allegiance to, or dependence upon, the crown or parliament of Great Britain; and that they give the assent of this colony to such declaration, and to whatever measures may be thought proper and necessary by the Congress for forming foreign alliances and a confederation of the colonies, at such time, and in the manner, as to them shall seem best: Provided, that the power of forming government for, and the regulations of the internal concerns of each colony, be left to the respective colonial legislatures.

Resolved unanimously, that a committee be appointed to prepare a Declaration of Rights, and such a plan of government as will be most likely to maintain peace and order in this colony, and secure substantial and equal liberty to the people.

Edm^{d} Pendleton P.

a Copy
John Tazewell
Clerk of the Convention.

10. *VIRGINIA'S RESOLUTION INSTRUCTING ITS DELEGATES TO MOVE FOR INDEPENDENCE*, May 15, 1776, Misc. PCC, RG 360. 14⅞ x 9⅛ in. *2 pages (page 2 illustrated). Endorsed: Instructions given by/the Convention of Virginia/to their delegates./read 27. May 1776./May 15th 1776.*

The Lee Resolution for Independence

On the morning of June 7, Richard Henry Lee, in compliance with the instructions of the Convention of Virginia, rose in Congress and offered this resolution:

> That these United Colonies are, and of right ought to be, free and independent States, that they are absolved from all allegiance to the British Crown, and that all political connection between them and the State of Great Britain is, and ought to be, totally dissolved. (Document 11.)

Congress deferred action on this resolution until the following day and then, after debate, until June 10.

Many members of Congress expressed opposition to the Lee Resolution; they believed a declaration of independence to be premature. Other delegates felt they should have instructions from their colonies before voting on a question so momentous. Under these circumstances, on June 10 final action on the resolution was again postponed, for 3 weeks. Congress did, however, decide that "in the mean time least any time sh^{d} be lost in case the Congress agree to this resolution a committee be appointed to prepare a Declaration to the effect of the said first resolution."

Resolved That these United Colonies are, and of right ought to be, free and independent States, that they are absolved from all allegiance to the British Crown, and that all political connection between them and the State of Great Britain is, and ought to be, totally dissolved.

That it is expedient forthwith to take the most effectual measures for forming foreign Alliances.

That a plan of confederation be prepared and transmitted to the respective Colonies for their consideration and approbation.

11. THE LEE RESOLUTION FOR INDEPENDENCE, *June 7, 1776, PCC No. 23, Other Reports of Committees of Congress, 1776-88, I: 11, RG 360. 10 x 8 in. 1 page. Endorsed: June 7, 1776. No 4/Resolutions moved/June 7th 1776./referred for consideration/till to morrow./ /respecting Independanc/of the U.S*

1776. June 11.

Resolved That the committee for preparing the declaration consist of five

The members chosen Mr Jefferson, Mr J. Adams, Mr Franklin, Mr Sherman & Mr R.R. Livingston

Resolved That a committee be appointed to prepare & digest the form of a confederation to be entered into between these colonies

That a committee be appointed to prepare a plan of treaties to be proposed to foreign powers.

12. APPOINTMENT OF THE COMMITTEE TO PREPARE THE DECLARATION, *June 11, 1776, PCC No. 2, IV: 567, RG 360. 12½ x 7¾ in. 1 page (excerpt illustrated).*

the Com.ee of the whole Congress to whom was referred the resolution and agreed the Declaration respecting independence. — 17

Resolved That these united colonies are and of right ought to be free and independant states; that they are absolved from all allegiance to the british crown and that all political connection between them and the state of great Britain is and ought to be totally dissolved

Report &c July 2. 1776.
No 5 The resolution for independancy
Agreed to July 2d 1776

13. *ADOPTION OF THE LEE RESOLUTION FOR INDEPENDENCE, July 2, 1776, PCC No. 23, I: 17, RG 360. 12⅜ x 7⅜ in. 1 page. This document is the favorable report of the committee to which the Lee Resolution was referred, with the affirmative votes of 12 colonies listed at the right. Endorsed: Report &c July 2. 1776./ No 5/The resolution for/independancy./Agreed to July 2d 1776.*

The committee of five elected to prepare the Declaration of Independence included Thomas Jefferson, John Adams, Benjamin Franklin, Roger Sherman, and Robert R. Livingston (document 12).

The Lee Resolution was again before Congress for action on July 1. After considerable debate, the resolution was passed on July 2 by the votes of 12 colonies (document 13). New York's delegation cast no vote until the newly-elected New York Convention upheld the Declaration on July 9.

The Lee Resolution contained three parts: a declaration of independence, the formation of foreign alliances to win independence, and "a plan of confederation" to create a viable nation from the 13 States after independence. It took the next 5 years to implement this tripartite resolution.

The Declaration of Independence

The first step in implementing the Lee Resolution was to issue the Declaration of Independence. Between June 11 and June 28 Jefferson drafted the Declaration, submitted the draft separately to Adams and Franklin, and then obtained the approval of the entire committee. The document was debated in Committee of the Whole for several days before it was "agreed to" on July 4. Then Congress ordered

> That the declaration be authenticated & printed.
>
> That the committee appointed to prepare the declaration superintend & correct the press.
>
> That copies of the declaration be sent to the several assemblies, conventions & committees or councils of safety and to the several commanding officers of the continental troops; that it be proclaimed in each of the united states & at the head of the army.

The first printing of the Declaration was delivered to Congress on July 5 by John Dunlap, a Philadelphia printer. The title is simply "A Declaration By the Representatives of the United States of America. In General Congress assembled," and below the text appears only the statement, "Signed by Order and in Behalf of the Congress, John Hancock, President. Attest. Charles Thomson, Secretary," and the colophon of John Dunlap, Philadelphia (document 14).

New York having approved the Declaration on July 9, Congress ordered on July 19 that the Declaration be engrossed on parchment with a new title, "The unanimous declaration of the thirteen united States of America," and "that the same when engrossed be signed by every member of Congress." The engrosser, probably Timothy Matlack, completed his work shortly thereafter, and "the declaration of independence being engrossed and compared at the table was signed" on August 2.

The printed copy of July 5 had borne only the name of John Hancock, President of the Congress, attested by Charles Thomson, Secretary. Hancock was the first to sign the engrossed parchment, in the center below the text. According to the custom of the time, the delegates began to sign at the right below the text, and their signatures were arranged according to the States they represented, beginning with the northernmost, New Hampshire, and ending with the southernmost, Georgia, at the left. Eventually 56 members of Congress affixed their signatures to the Declaration, though not all were present on August 2. As delegates who had been absent returned to Congress they signed the document. A few delegates, either from conviction or from negligence, did not sign at all.

The signers' names were not made public for some time, apparently because of the possibility of reprisal against individuals, who, in the eyes of Great Britain, were rebels and traitors. After Washington's victories at Trenton and Princeton, however, Congress on January 18, 1777, ordered that "an authenticated copy of the Declaration of Independency with the names of the members of Congress subscribing the same be sent to each of the United States."

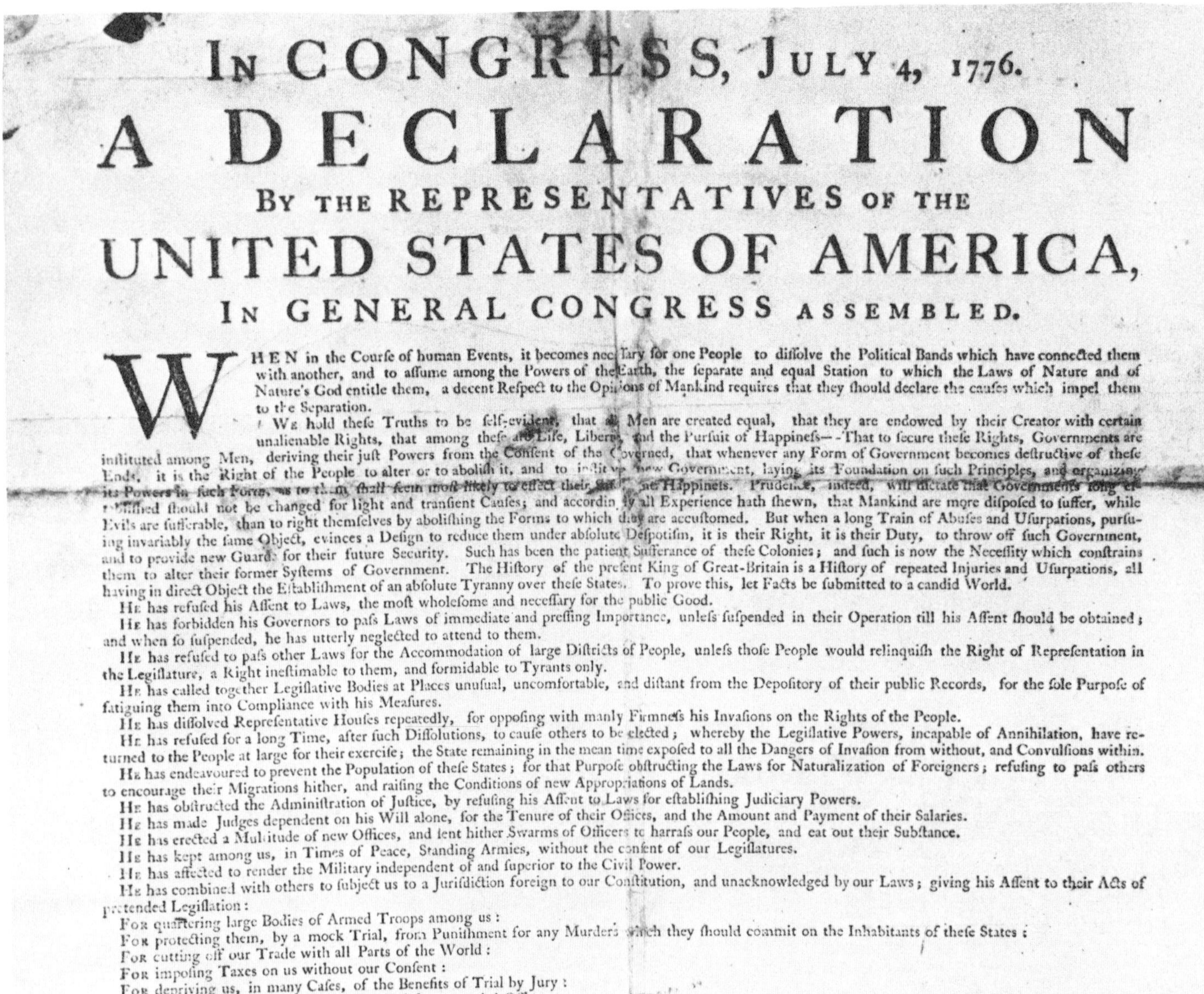

IN CONGRESS, JULY 4, 1776.

A DECLARATION

BY THE REPRESENTATIVES OF THE UNITED STATES OF AMERICA, IN GENERAL CONGRESS ASSEMBLED.

WHEN in the Courſe of human Events, it becomes neceſſary for one People to diſſolve the Political Bands which have connected them with another, and to aſſume among the Powers of the Earth, the ſeparate and equal Station to which the Laws of Nature and of Nature's God entitle them, a decent Reſpect to the Opinions of Mankind requires that they ſhould declare the cauſes which impel them to the Separation.

We hold theſe Truths to be ſelf-evident, that all Men are created equal, that they are endowed by their Creator with certain unalienable Rights, that among theſe are Life, Liberty, and the Purſuit of Happineſs—That to ſecure theſe Rights, Governments are inſtituted among Men, deriving their juſt Powers from the Conſent of the Governed, that whenever any Form of Government becomes deſtructive of theſe Ends, it is the Right of the People to alter or to aboliſh it, and to inſtitute new Government, laying its Foundation on ſuch Principles, and organizing its Powers in ſuch Form, as to them ſhall ſeem moſt likely to effect their Safety and Happineſs. Prudence, indeed, will dictate that Governments long eſtabliſhed ſhould not be changed for light and tranſient Cauſes; and accordingly all Experience hath ſhewn, that Mankind are more diſpoſed to ſuffer, while Evils are ſufferable, than to right themſelves by aboliſhing the Forms to which they are accuſtomed. But when a long Train of Abuſes and Uſurpations, purſuing invariably the ſame Object, evinces a Deſign to reduce them under abſolute Deſpotiſm, it is their Right, it is their Duty, to throw off ſuch Government, and to provide new Guards for their future Security. Such has been the patient Sufferance of theſe Colonies; and ſuch is now the Neceſſity which conſtrains them to alter their former Syſtems of Government. The Hiſtory of the preſent King of Great-Britain is a Hiſtory of repeated Injuries and Uſurpations, all having in direct Object the Eſtabliſhment of an abſolute Tyranny over theſe States. To prove this, let Facts be ſubmitted to a candid World.

HE has refuſed his Aſſent to Laws, the moſt wholeſome and neceſſary for the public Good.

HE has forbidden his Governors to paſs Laws of immediate and preſſing Importance, unleſs ſuſpended in their Operation till his Aſſent ſhould be obtained; and when ſo ſuſpended, he has utterly neglected to attend to them.

HE has refuſed to paſs other Laws for the Accommodation of large Diſtricts of People, unleſs thoſe People would relinquiſh the Right of Repreſentation in the Legiſlature, a Right ineſtimable to them, and formidable to Tyrants only.

HE has called together Legiſlative Bodies at Places unuſual, uncomfortable, and diſtant from the Depoſitory of their public Records, for the ſole Purpoſe of fatiguing them into Compliance with his Meaſures.

HE has diſſolved Repreſentative Houſes repeatedly, for oppoſing with manly Firmneſs his Invaſions on the Rights of the People.

HE has refuſed for a long Time, after ſuch Diſſolutions, to cauſe others to be elected; whereby the Legiſlative Powers, incapable of Annihilation, have returned to the People at large for their exerciſe; the State remaining in the mean time expoſed to all the Dangers of Invaſion from without, and Convulſions within.

HE has endeavoured to prevent the Population of theſe States; for that Purpoſe obſtructing the Laws for Naturalization of Foreigners; refuſing to paſs others to encourage their Migrations hither, and raiſing the Conditions of new Appropriations of Lands.

HE has obſtructed the Adminiſtration of Juſtice, by refuſing his Aſſent to Laws for eſtabliſhing Judiciary Powers.

HE has made Judges dependent on his Will alone, for the Tenure of their Offices, and the Amount and Payment of their Salaries.

HE has erected a Multitude of new Offices, and ſent hither Swarms of Officers to harraſs our People, and eat out their Subſtance.

HE has kept among us, in Times of Peace, Standing Armies, without the conſent of our Legiſlatures.

HE has affected to render the Military independent of and ſuperior to the Civil Power.

HE has combined with others to ſubject us to a Juriſdiction foreign to our Conſtitution, and unacknowledged by our Laws; giving his Aſſent to their Acts of pretended Legiſlation:

FOR quartering large Bodies of Armed Troops among us:

FOR protecting them, by a mock Trial, from Puniſhment for any Murders which they ſhould commit on the Inhabitants of theſe States:

FOR cutting off our Trade with all Parts of the World:

FOR impoſing Taxes on us without our Conſent:

FOR depriving us, in many Caſes, of the Benefits of Trial by Jury:

FOR tranſporting us beyond Seas to be tried for pretended Offences:

FOR aboliſhing the free Syſtem of Engliſh Laws in a neighbouring Province, eſtabliſhing therein an arbitrary Government, and enlarging its Boundaries, ſo as to render it at once an Example and fit Inſtrument for introducing the ſame abſolute Rule into theſe Colonies:

FOR taking away our Charters, aboliſhing our moſt valuable Laws, and altering fundamentally the Forms of our Governments:

FOR ſuſpending our own Legiſlatures, and declaring themſelves inveſted with Power to legiſlate for us in all Caſes whatſoever.

HE has abdicated Government here, by declaring us out of his Protection and waging War againſt us.

HE has plundered our Seas, ravaged our Coaſts, burnt our Towns, and deſtroyed the Lives of our People.

HE is, at this Time, tranſporting large Armies of foreign Mercenaries to compleat the Works of Death, Deſolation, and Tyranny, already begun with circumſtances of Cruelty and Perfidy, ſcarcely paralleled in the moſt barbarous Ages, and totally unworthy the Head of a civilized Nation.

HE has conſtrained our fellow Citizens taken Captive on the high Seas to bear Arms againſt their Country, to become the Executioners of their Friends and Brethren, or to fall themſelves by their Hands.

HE has excited domeſtic Inſurrections amongſt us, and has endeavoured to bring on the Inhabitants of our Frontiers, the mercileſs Indian Savages, whoſe known Rule of Warfare, is an undiſtinguiſhed Deſtruction, of all Ages, Sexes and Conditions.

IN every ſtage of theſe Oppreſſions we have Petitioned for Redreſs in the moſt humble Terms: Our repeated Petitions have been anſwered only by repeated Injury. A Prince, whoſe Character is thus marked by every act which may define a Tyrant, is unfit to be the Ruler of a free People.

NOR have we been wanting in Attentions to our Britiſh Brethren. We have warned them from Time to Time of Attempts by their Legiſlature to extend an unwarrantable Juriſdiction over us. We have reminded them of the Circumſtances of our Emigration and Settlement here. We have appealed to their native Juſtice and Magnanimity, and we have conjured them by the Ties of our common Kindred to diſavow theſe Uſurpations, which, would inevitably interrupt our Connections and Correſpondence. They too have been deaf to the Voice of Juſtice and of Conſanguinity. We muſt, therefore, acquieſce in the Neceſſity, which denounces our Separation, and hold them, as we hold the reſt of Mankind, Enemies in War, in Peace, Friends.

WE, therefore, the Repreſentatives of the UNITED STATES OF AMERICA, in GENERAL CONGRESS, Aſſembled, appealing to the Supreme Judge of the World for the Rectitude of our Intentions, do, in the Name, and by Authority of the good People of theſe Colonies, ſolemnly Publiſh and Declare, That theſe United Colonies are, and of Right ought to be, FREE AND INDEPENDENT STATES; that they are abſolved from all Allegiance to the Britiſh Crown, and that all political Connection between them and the State of Great-Britain, is and ought to be totally diſſolved; and that as FREE AND INDEPENDENT STATES, they have full Power to levy War, conclude Peace, contract Alliances, eſtabliſh Commerce, and to do all other Acts and Things which INDEPENDENT STATES may of right do. And for the ſupport of this Declaration, with a firm Reliance on the Protection of divine Providence, we mutually pledge to each other our Lives, our Fortunes, and our ſacred Honor.

Signed by ORDER *and in* BEHALF *of the* CONGRESS,

JOHN HANCOCK, PRESIDENT.

ATTEST.
CHARLES THOMSON, SECRETARY.

PHILADELPHIA: PRINTED BY JOHN DUNLAP.

14. FIRST PRINTING OF THE DECLARATION OF INDEPENDENCE, July 4, 1776, PCC No. 1, III: 94, RG 360. 18 x 14¾ in. Broadside. Printed by John Dunlap, Philadelphia. Wafered into the Rough Journal of the Congress for July 4.

The First Foreign Alliance

Although the need for foreign aid was agreed upon in the Lee Resolution, the attempt to form foreign alliances was undertaken only after serious deliberation and weighing all foreseeable consequences. Therefore, a great deal of thought was given to the terms which the United States would be willing to accept in order to obtain alliances and commercial treaties. Benjamin Franklin, who had spent many years in England as a colonial agent, was a logical choice to be a member of a committee to draw up a "Plan of Treaties" (document 15); also on the committee were John Adams, Benjamin Harrison, John Dickinson, and Robert Morris.

The "Plan of 1776," adopted in September on the recommendation of this committee, was a model treaty to be used by agents of the United States when they approached European nations to negotiate treaties. All but one of the commercial treaties which the United States entered into during the 19th century were patterned after this plan.

Under detailed instructions from the Continental Congress, a three-man commission consisting of Benjamin Franklin, Silas Deane and Arthur Lee was assigned the task of negotiating treaties of commerce with other powers. At first the representatives were not instructed to seek military alliances, so averse was the Congress to becoming involved in future European wars; but this limitation was shortly lifted.

France was favorably disposed toward the Americans even before Franklin arrived in Paris. At the end of the French and Indian War in 1763, France, shorn of most of its empire, was overshadowed by Great Britain in every European chancellery. Humiliated, the French bided their time, hoping for revenge. They watched with interest the growing friction between Great Britain and the American colonies and the outbreak of revolution. In 1776, even before the colonies had declared their independence, France had secretly begun to supply them with aid, through a fictitious company headed by the romantic playwright, pœt, and courtier, Pierre Augustin Caron de Beaumarchais. It was not, however, until the American victory in the Saratoga campaign that the French agreed to negotiate with the American diplomats as envoys of an independent power.

The British plan of campaign for 1777 was to cut off New England from the other States; General Sir William Howe was to ascend the Hudson River from New York and General John Burgoyne was to proceed from Canada to meet him. The plan failed when the Americans under General Horatio Gates decisively defeated General Burgoyne's veteran troops near Saratoga on October 17 and forced his surrender. On the 18th, Gates proudly transmitted to Congress a copy of the generous surrender terms signed by Burgoyne (document 16).

This great Saratoga victory finally convinced France that an open military alliance with the United States would not be too much of a risk militarily and must be pushed through quickly if France was to reap benefits from the Anglo-American conflict. The Comte de Vergennes, the French foreign minister, was thoroughly alarmed when Benjamin Franklin informed him that the British Ministry was making unofficial conciliatory overtures to the American diplomats in France. Vergennes used this information to convince King Louis XVI and the rest of his ministers that it was essential for France to recognize the independence of the United States and enter into a formal alliance with the new nation if Great Britain was to be prevented from regaining her American empire.

On February 6, 1778, in Paris, Franklin, Deane, and Lee signed two pacts with the French. One was a treaty of commerce with terms almost identical to those specified by Congress in the Plan of 1776. The other was a military alliance (document 17). Not only the American determination to be free, but the compelling French resolution as well that Britain should be shorn of her colonies, is demonstrated in two important articles:

> Art. 2. The essential and direct End of the present defensive alliance is to maintain effectually the liberty, Sovereignty, and independance absolute and unlimited of the said united States. . . .
>
> Art. 8. Neither of the two Parties Shall conclude either Truce or Peace with Great Britain . . . until the Independence of the united States Shall have been formally or tacitly assured by the Treaty or Treaties that shall terminate the War.

The military stores which had been secretly supplied by Beaumarchais helped to make the Saratoga victory possible, and the arrival of the gallant young Marquis de Lafayette in April 1777 as a volunteer in the cause of American freedom gave the army a dedicated leader. But the solid support of the professional army of Louis XVI under the command of the Comte de Rochambeau and the French Navy under Admiral de Grasse, sent to fulfill the terms of the Alliance of 1778, contributed more to the final victory for American independence.

The French alliance was the only military alliance made by the United States until it joined the United Nations in 1942.

129

Coll. of State Tracts 109
Coll. of Sea Laws 541.

There Shall be a firm, inviolable, and universal Peace, and a true and Sincere Friendship between the most Serene and mighty Prince, Lewis the Sixteenth, the most Christian King his Heirs and Successors, and the united States of America; and the Subjects of the most Christian King, and of the Said States; and between the Countries, Islands, Cities, and Towns Situate under the Jurisdiction of the most Christian King and of the Said united States, ~~and every of them~~, and the People and Inhabitants thereof of every degree; without Exception of Persons or Places; and the Terms hereinafter mentioned Shall be perpetual between the most Christian King, his Heirs and Successors, and the Said united States.

Art. 1. The Subjects of the most Christian King Shall pay no other Duties or Imposts in the Ports, Havens, Roads, Countries, Islands, Cities, or Towns of the Said united States, or any of them, than the Natives thereof, or any Commercial Companies established by them or any of them, Shall pay, but Shall enjoy all other the Rights, Liberties, Priviledges, Immunities, and Exemptions in Trade, Navigation and Commerce in passing from one Part thereof to another, and in going to and from the Same, from and to any Part of the World, which the Said Natives, or Companies enjoy.

ag.

Art. 2. The Subjects, People and Inhabitants of the Said united States and every of them Shall pay no other Duties, or Imposts in the Ports, Havens, Roads, Countries, Islands, Cities, or Towns of the most Christian King, than the Natives of such Countries, Islands, Cities, or Towns of France, or any commercial Companies established by the most Christian King Shall pay, but Shall enjoy all other the Rights, Liberties, Priviledges, Immunities and Exemptions in Trade, Navigation and Commerce, in passing from one Part thereof to another, and in going to and from the Same, from and to any Part of the World, which the Said Natives, or Companies enjoy.

Should there not be an exception of Asia, and perhaps of Africa.–

ag.

15A. "PLAN OF TREATIES," ADAMS' DRAFT, PCC No. 47, *Articles of Confederation, With Plans and Drafts of Treaties and Other Miscellaneous Papers, 1775-84, pp. 129-135, RG 360. 12½ x 8 in. In the hand of John Adams, a member of the Committee Appointed to Prepare a Plan of Treaties, with marginal notes indicating the sources he had consulted and the action of the Congress on each proposed Article. 6 pages and endorsement (page 129 illustrated). Endorsed: Plan of Treaties.*

[1]

THERE ſhall be a firm, inviolable, and univerſal peace, and a true and ſincere friendſhip between A. and B. and the ſubjects of A. and of B. and between the countries, iſlands, cities and towns ſituate under the juriſdiction of A. and of B. and the people and inhabitants thereof of every degree, without exception of perſons or places; and the Terms herein after mentioned ſhall be perpetual between A. and B.

I. The ſubjects of A. ſhall pay no other duties or impoſts in the ports, havens, roads, countries, iſlands, cities or towns of B. than the natives thereof or any commercial Companies eſtabliſhed therein ſhall pay, but ſhall enjoy all other the rights, liberties, privileges, immunities and exemptions in trade navigation and commerce, in paſſing from one part thereof to another, and in going to and from the ſame, from and to any part of the world, which the ſaid natives or Companies enjoy.

II. The ſubjects of B. ſhall pay no other duties or impoſts in the ports, havens, roads, countries, iſlands, cities or towns of A. than the natives thereof or any commercial Companies eſtabliſhed therein; but ſhall enjoy all other the rights, liberties, privileges, immunities and exemptions in trade, navigation and commerce in paſſing from one part thereof to another, and in going to and from the ſame from and to any part of the world, which the ſaid natives or Companies enjoy.

+

III. A. ſhall endeavour by all the means in his power to protect and defend all veſſels and the effects belonging to the ſubjects and people of B. being in his ports, havens or roads, or on the ſeas, or near to his countries, iſlands, cities or towns, and to recover and reſtore to the right owners, their agents or attornies, all ſuch veſſels and effects which ſhall be taken within his juriſdiction; and his ſhips of war or any convoys ſailing under his authority ſhall upon all occaſions take under their protection all veſſels belonging to the ſubjects or people of B. and holding the ſame courſe or going the ſame way, and ſhall defend ſuch veſſels ſo long as they hold the ſame courſe or go the ſame way againſt all attacks, force and violence, in the ſame manner as they ought to protect and defend veſſels belonging to the ſubjects or people of A.

IV. In like manner B. and his ſhips of war, and convoys, ſailing under his authority, ſhall protect and defend all veſſels and effects belonging to the ſubjects or people of A. and endeavour to recover and reſtore them, if taken within his juriſdiction.

V. A. and B. ſhall not receive nor ſuffer to be received into any of their ports, havens, roads, countries, iſlands, cities or towns, any pirates or ſea robbers, or afford or ſuffer any entertainment, aſſiſtance or proviſion to be afforded to them, but ſhall endeavour by all means that all pirates and ſea robbers and their partners, ſharers and abettors be found out, apprehended and ſuffer condign puniſhment; and all the veſſels and effects piratically taken and brought into the ports or havens of A. or B. which can be found, altho' they be ſold, ſhall be reſtored or ſatiſfaction given therefor to the right owners, their agents or attornies demanding the ſame and making the right of property to appear by due proof.

N. If France should undertake an Expedition to recover what she lost in the West Indies during the last War with G. Britain, we will in that Expedition supply France with Provisions, and refuse to supply any to G. Britain

VI. A. ſhall protect, defend and ſecure, as far as in his power the ſubjects or people of B. and their veſſels and effects of every kind, againſt all attacks, aſſaults, violences, injuries, depredations or plunderings by or from the King or Emperor of Morocco or Fez, and the States of Algiers, Tunis and Tripoli, and any of them, and every other prince, ſtate and power on the coaſt of Barbary in Africa, and the ſubjects of the ſaid Kings, Emperors, &c. in as full a manner, &c.

+ Qu. whether it would not be proper if it should be insisted upon to accede to an exclusive Contract during the war for Masts all naval Stores, as far as we can spare them.

✕

VII. If, in conſequence of this Treaty, the —— of —— ſhould declare war againſt A. the ſaid B. ſhall not aſſiſt —— with men, money, ſhips, or any of the articles in this Treaty denominated contraband goods, ~~or in any other way. And if A. to favor the ſaid B. ſhall join in the preſent war againſt ——, A ſhall not make a ſeparate peace.~~

Labrador New Britain Nova Scotia Acadia Canada Florida

VIII. In caſe of any war between A. and ——, A ſhall never invade, nor attempt to invade or get poſſeſſion for himſelf of ——, nor any of the countries, cities or towns on the Continent of ——, nor of the Iſlands of —— nor any other iſland lying near to the ſaid Continent, in the ſeas, or in any gulph, bay, or river thereof, it being the true intent and meaning of this Treaty, that the ſaid B. ſhall have the ſole, excluſive, undivided and perpetual poſſeſſion of all the countries, cities and towns on the ſaid Continent, and of all iſlands near to it, whenever ~~the ſame can be invaded and conquered by B, or ſhall in any manner ſubmit to or~~ be confederated with B. That A. shall retain the same Rights of Fishery on the Banks of Newfoundland and all other Rights relating to any of the Islands which she is entitled to by Virtue of the Treaty of Paris

Newfoundland Cape Breton St Johns Anticosti Bermudas nor Bahama Islands

Qu. whether it will not be proper to engage that the United States will not stipulate in favour of G. Britain upon a Peace with her Terms of Commerce more advantageous than they will stipulate in favour of France

+ The 22d Article comes in here

15B. "PLAN OF TREATIES," REPORT OF THE COMMITTEE APPOINTED TO PREPARE A PLAN OF TREATIES, *July 18, 1776, PCC No. 47, pp. 161-165, RG 360. 12⅞ x 8¼ in. Printed report with marginal notes in the hand of James Wilson of Pennsylvania. 5 pages (page 161 illustrated).*

278

Camp at Saratoga 18th Octr 1777.

Sir

I have the Satisfaction to present Your Excellency with The Convention of Saratoga By which His Excellency Lieutenant General Burgoyne, has Surrendered Himself, & his whole Army into my Hands, & they are now upon Their March to Boston. This Signal, and Important Event, is the more Glorious, as it was Effected with so little loss to the Army of The United States.

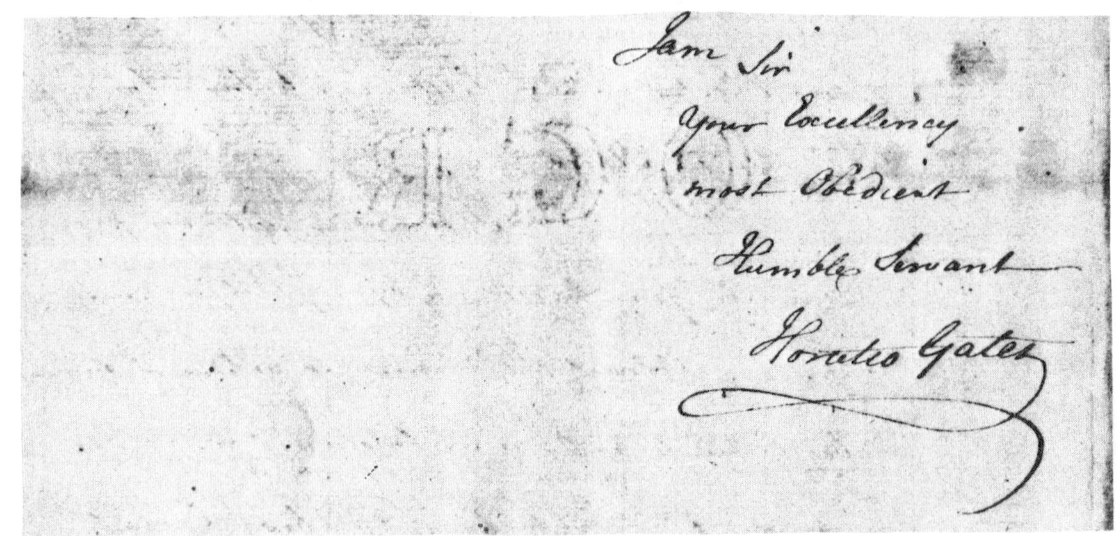

I am Sir
Your Excellency
most Obedient
Humble Servant
Horatio Gates

16. *GENERAL GATES' ANNOUNCEMENT OF BURGOYNE'S SURRENDER AT SARATOGA, October 18, 1777, PCC No. 154, Letters from Maj. Gen. Horatio Gates, 1775-82, I: 278-279, RG 360. 12¾ x 7⅝ in. Signed by General Gates with surrender terms enclosed. 2 pages (1 page and signature of letter illustrated). Letter endorsed: No 32/Letter from genl Gates/Saratoga Octr 18. 1777/with copy of convention/(read the 31st). Surrender terms endorsed: Copy Capitulation/between M. Genl Gates/& Lt Genl Burgoyne/Dated Saratoga Octr 16th 1777.*

Treaty of Alliance

The most Christian King and the United States of North America, to wit, New hampshire, Massachusetts Bay, Rhodeisland, Connecticut, Newyork, New Jersey, Pennsylvania, Delaware, Maryland, Virginia, North Carolina, South Carolina, and Georgia, having this Day concluded a Treaty of amity and Commerce, for the reciprocal advantage of their Subjects and Citizens have thought it necessary to take into consideration the means of Strengthening those engagements and of rondring them useful to the safety and tranquility of the two parties, particulary in case Great Britain in Resentment of that connection and of the good correspon-dence which is the object of the Said Treaty should break the Peace with france, either by direct hostilities, or by hindring her commerce and navigation, in a manner contrary to the Rights of Nations, and the Peace subsisting between the two Crowns; and his Majesty and the Said united States having resolved in that Case to join their Councils and efforts against the Enterprises of their common Enemy, the respective Plenipotentiaries, impowerd to concert the Clauses & conditions proper to fulfil the said

Traité d'alliance éventuelle et déffensive

Le Roi Très Chretien et les Etats-unis de l'Amerique Septentrionale, savoir New-hampshire, la Baye de Massachuset, Rhode-Island Connecticut, Newyork, New-Jersey, Pensylvanie, Delaware, Maryland, Virginie, Caroline Septentrionale, Caroline Meridionale et Georgie, ayant conclu ce jourd'huy un Traité d'amitie, de bonne intelligence et de commerce, pour l'avantage reciproque de leurs Sujets et Citoyens, ils ont cru devoir prendre en consideration les moyens de resserrer leurs liaisons, et de les rendre utiles à la Sureté et à la tranquilité des deux Parties, notamment dans le cas où la grande Bretagne, en haine de ces mêmes liaisons et de la bonne correspondance qui forment l'objet du dit Traité, se porteroit à rompre la paix avec la france, soit en l'attaquant hostilement, soit en troublant son commerce et sa navigation, d'une maniere contraire au droit des gens et à la paix subsistante entre les deux Couronnes; et Sa Majesté

17. *THE TREATY OF ALLIANCE WITH FRANCE*, February 6, 1778, American Original, Treaty Series No. 82, RG 11, General Records of the United States Government. 15⅝ x 10½ in. 7 pages (pages 1 and 7 illustrated). Text in French and in English.

Intentions, have after the most mature Deliberation, concluded and determined on the following Articles.

Art. 1.

If War should break out betwan France and Great Britain, during the continuence of the present War betwan the United States and England, his Majesty and the said united States, shall make it a common cause, and aid each other mutually with their good Offices their Counsels, and their forces, according to the exigence of Conjunctures as becomes good & faithful Allies.

Art. 2.

The essential and direct End of the present defensive alliance is to maintain effectually the liberty, Sovereignty, and independance absolute and unlimited of the said united States, as well in Matters of Gouvernement as of commerce.

Art. 3.

The two contracting Parties shall each on its own Part, and in the manner it may judge most proper, make all the

et les dits Etats unis ayant résolu éventuellement d'unir, dans le cas prévu, leurs conseils et leurs efforts contre les entreprises de leur ennemi commun, les Plenipotentiaires respectifs, chargés de concerter les clauses et conditions propres à remplir leurs intentions, ont, après la plus mure délibération, conclu et arresté les points et articles qui s'ensuivent.

Article premier.

Si la guerre éclate entre la france et la Grande Brétagne, pendant la durée de la guerre actuelle entre les Etats unis et l'Angleterre, Sa Majesté et les dits Etats-unis feront cause commune et s'entraideront mutuellement de leurs bons offices, de leurs conseils et de leurs forces, selon l'exigence des conjonctures, ainsy qu'il convient à de bons et fideles Alliés.

Article Second.

Le but essentiel et direct de la présente alliance deffensive, est de maintenir efficacement la liberté, la Souveraineté, et l'independance absolue et illimitée des dits Etats unis, tant en matière politique que de commerce.

Article trois.

Les deux Parties contractantes feront chacune de leur côté, et de la manière qu'elles jugeront plus convenable, tous

(Continuation of Document 17)

sooner if possible.

In faith whereof the respective Plenipotentiaries, to wit on the part of the most Christian King Conrad Alexander Gerard royal Syndic of the City of Strasbourgh & Secretary of his Majesty's Council of State and on the part of the United States Benjamin Franklin Deputy to the General Congress from the State of Pensylvania and President of the Convention of the same State, Silas Deane heretofore Deputy from the State of Connecticut & Arthur Lee Councellor at Law have signed the above Articles both in the French and English Languages declaring Nevertheless that the present Treaty was originally composed and concluded in the French Language, and they have hereunto affixed their Seals

Done at Paris, this sixth Day of February one thousand seven hundred and seventy eight.

C.A. Gerard B Franklin

six mois ou plutôt, si faire se peut.

En foi de quoi les Plenipotentiaires respectifs, savoir de la part du Roi Très Chrétien le Sr. Conrad Alexandre Gerard Sindic royal de la ville de Strasbourg et Secrétaire du Conseil d'Etat de Sa Majesté, et de la part des Etats unis les Srs. Benjamin Franklin Député au Congrès général de la part de l'Etat de Pensylvanie et President de la Convention du meme Etat, Silas Deane cy devant Député de l'Etat de Connecticut et Arthur Lee Conseiller ès loix ont signé les articles ci dessus, tant en langue françoise qu'en langue angloise, déclarant néanmoins que le present traité a été originairement redigé et arrêté en langue françoise, et ils les ont munis du cachet de leurs armes.

Fait à Paris le sixieme jour du mois de Fevrier mil sept cent soixante dix huit.

Silas Deane Arthur Lee

A Plan of Confederation

On the same June day in 1776 when the Continental Congress appointed a committee to draft a declaration of independence and another to prepare a plan of treaties, it also decided to appoint a committee to implement the third part of the Lee Resolution, "to prepare and digest the form of a confederation to be entered into between these colonies."

This was not the first time confederation had been proposed in the Continental Congress. In the First Continental Congress, Joseph Galloway, a conservative merchant from Philadelphia desperately anxious to heal the breach between Great Britain and her colonies, proposed a plan of union which would have made a permanent institution of an American Congress and carefully defined its relationship to the British Parliament. Galloway's plan was rejected, and no record of it was entered in the Journal of the Congress.

Again in July 1775, a year before independence was declared, Benjamin Franklin outlined a plan of union. Although it was entitled "Articles of Confederation and Perpetual Union," it made a conciliatory gesture toward Great Britain in providing for a temporary confederation until Britain's differences with the American colonies were reconciled. Only if reconciliation failed would confederation become permanent. The plan for a confederacy, to be called the United Colonies of North America, would have established an elected assembly with power to declare war, form alliances, appoint ambassadors, control the armed forces, settle intercolonial disputes, and deal with general questions of trade. Expenses would have been met from a common treasury, supplied by funds from the Colonies, whose legislatures would have had the sole right to levy taxes. Congress, however, was not yet ready for any plan of confederation and Franklin's scheme was forgotten for nearly a year.

Once independence was under serious consideration, however, a committee made up of one member from each of the Thirteen Colonies was named to determine the form of a confederation. John Dickinson, who dominated the committee, had become famous in 1768 as the writer of *Letters from a Farmer in Pennsylvania to the Inhabitants of the British Colonies* protesting the taxes imposed by the Townshend Acts on the grounds that Parliament had no authority to tax the colonies in any way. In 1776 he was a delegate from Delaware.

The Dickinson Draft of the Articles of Confederation (document 18) was ready for consideration on July 12. Article I stated:

> The name of this Confederacy shall be "The United States of America."

It provided for a Congress in which each State was represented in proportion to its population, but the smaller States were strongly opposed to this system. There was also vigorous resistance to the clause of the Dickinson Draft which would have assigned to the national government all powers not specifically reserved to the States. Having just declared themselves independent of a distant centralized control by King and Parliament, the new States were not yet ready to create a strong central government in America.

It was not until July 9, 1778, that the final form of the Articles of Confederation was accepted and an engrossed copy (document 19) was prepared for signature by the delegates. Eight States had instructed their delegates to sign the Articles by that day; on February 22, 1779, when Delaware's delegates signed, all the States but Maryland had ratified the agreement for confederation.

Sometimes called "the first constitution of the United States," the Articles of Confederation were in many ways more like a treaty among a group of small nations than a true frame of government. Each State expressly retained

> its sovereignty, freedom and independence, and every Power, Jurisdiction and right, . . . not by this confederation expressly delegated to the United States, in Congress assembled.

Every State had one vote in Congress, regardless of its geographic area or population. Congress was legally given the powers it had been exercising during its existence since 1775: the "United States in Congress assembled" could make war and peace, send and receive ambassadors, enter into treaties and alliances, coin money, regulate Indian affairs, and establish a post office. It could not levy taxes or regulate commerce. There was no national executive and no system of national courts. The Articles could be amended only by unanimous vote, and the Confederation was not to come into being until all 13 States had ratified.

Maryland's ratification was withheld until February 2, 1781. A small State cut off from expansion to the West by the territory of Virginia and Pennsylvania, Maryland was apprehensive about joining a confederation in which some States claimed land extending to the Mississippi River, or even to the Pacific. Gradually, other States bowed to Maryland's insistence. In 1780, New York ceded her western land claims to the United States, and Congress in accepting them passed a very important

Articles of Confederation and perpetual Union between the Colonies [States] of New Hampshire &c at Philadelphia the Day of 1776

Art. 1 The Name of this Confederacy shall be "The United States of America."

Art. 2d The said Colonies [States] unite themselves so as never to be divided by any Act whatever, and hereby severally enter into a firm League of Friendship with each other, for their common Defence, the Security of their Liberties, and their mutual and general Welfare, binding the said Colonies [themselves] to assist one [each] another against all Force offered to or Attacks made upon them or any of them, on Account of Religion, Sovereignty, Trade, or any other Pretence whatever.

agreed.

Q. Should not the first Article provide for a Toleration and agt. Establishments hereafter to be made?

Art. 3d Each Colony [State] shall retain and enjoy as much of its present Laws, Rights and Customs as it may think fit, and reserves to itself the sole and exclusive Regulation and Government of its internal Police, in all Matters that shall not interfere with the Articles of this Confederation.

18. *THE ARTICLES OF CONFEDERATION: DICKINSON'S DRAFT, July 12, 1776, PCC No. 47, pp. 9-20, RG 360. 12½ x 8 in. In the hand of John Dickinson. 12 pages (page 1 illustrated). Endorsed: Report of Articles/of Confederation/in the handwriting of/Mr J. Dickinson/The comee Mr Bartlet/ Mr S. Adams/Mr Hopkins/Mr Sherman/Mr R R Livingston/Mr Dickinson/Mr McKean/Mr Stone/Mr Nelson/Mr Hewes/Mr E. Rutlidge/Mr Gwinnet/ appd 12 June 1776/Delivered/July 12. 1776*

To all to whom

these Presents shall come, we the under signed Delegates of the States affixed to our Names send greeting. Whereas the Delegates of the United States of America in Congress assembled did on the fifteenth day of November in the Year of our Lord One Thousand Seven Hundred and Seventy seven, and in the Second Year of the Independence of America agree to certain articles of Confederation and perpetual Union between the States of Newhampshire, Massachusetts-bay, Rhodeisland and Providence Plantations, Connecticut, New York, New Jersey, Pennsylvania, Delaware, Maryland, Virginia, North Carolina, South Carolina and Georgia in the Words following, viz. "Articles of Confederation and perpetual Union between the states of Newhampshire, Massachusetts-bay, Rhodeisland and Providence Plantations, Connecticut, New-York, New-Jersey, Pennsylvania, Delaware, Maryland, Virginia, North-Carolina, South-Carolina and Georgia.

Article I. The Stile of this confederacy shall be "The United States of America."

Article II. Each state retains its sovereignty, freedom and independence, and every Power, Jurisdiction and right, which is not by this confederation expressly delegated to the United States, in Congress assembled.

Article III. The said states hereby severally enter into a firm league of friendship with each other, for their common defence, the security of their Liberties, and their mutual and general welfare, binding themselves to assist each other, against all force offered to, or attacks made upon them, or any of them, on account of religion, sovereignty, trade, or any other pretence whatever.

Article IV. The better to secure and perpetuate mutual friendship and intercourse among the people of the different states in this union, the free inhabitants of each of these states, paupers, vagabonds and fugitives from Justice excepted, shall be entitled to all privileges and immunities of free citizens in the several states; and the people of each state shall have free ingress and regress to and from any other state, and shall enjoy therein all the privileges of trade and commerce, subject to the same duties, impositions and restrictions as the inhabitants thereof respectively, provided

19. *THE ENGROSSED ARTICLES OF CONFEDERATION, July 9, 1778, PCC No. 47, RG 360. 23½ x 15⅜ in. Document eventually signed by delegates from 13 States. Parchment sheets stitched together and fastened to a wooden roller. 6 pages, (parts of pages 1 and 6 illustrated). Endorsed:* Act of Confederation/of/ The United States of America.

any alteration at any time hereafter be made in any of them; unless such alteration be agreed to in a congress of the united states, and be afterwards confirmed by the legislatures of every state.

And Whereas it hath pleased the Great Governor of the World to incline the hearts of the legislatures we respectively represent in congress, to approve of, and to authorize us to ratify the said articles of confederation and perpetual union. **Know Ye** that we the under-signed delegates, by virtue of the power and authority to us given for that purpose, do by these presents, in the name and in behalf of our respective constituents, fully and entirely ratify and confirm each and every of the said articles of confederation and perpetual union, and all and singular the matters and things therein contained: And we do further solemnly plight and engage the faith of our respective constituents, that they shall abide by the determinations of the united states in congress assembled on all questions, which by the said confederation are submitted to them.

And that the articles thereof shall be inviolably observed by the states we respectively represent, and that the union shall be perpetual. In Witness whereof we have hereunto set our hands in Congress. Done at Philadelphia in the state of Pennsylvania the ninth Day of July in the Year of our Lord one thousand seven Hundred and Seventy-eight, and in the third year of the independence of America.

On the part & behalf of the State of Delaware: Tho M:Kean [illegible] 1779; John Dickinson May 5th 1779; Nicholas Van Dyke.

Josiah Bartlett; John Wentworth Junr August 8th 1778 — On the part & behalf of the State of New Hampshire

On the part and behalf of the State of Maryland: [illegible] March 1 1781; [illegible]

John Hancock

On the part and behalf of the State of Virginia: Richard Henry Lee; John Banister; Thomas Adams; Jno Harvie; Francis Lightfoot Lee

Samuel Adams; Elbridge Gerry; Francis Dana; James Lovell; Samuel Holten — On the part and behalf of the State of Massachusetts Bay

On the part and [illegible]: John Penn July 21 1778

resolution (document 20). Rejecting a colonial system for lands to be acquired by the United States, it declared that these lands

> shall be disposed of for the common benefit of the United States and be settled and formed into distinct republican States which shall become members of the fœderal Union and have the same rights of Sovereignty freedom and independence as the other states.

Only after Virginia ceded her claims on January 2, 1781, was Maryland willing to ratify the Articles of Confederation. At last the Second Continental Congress ended its long extra-legal status and became the Congress of the Confederation.

1780
Oct: 10

Resolved that the unappropriated lands that may be ceded or relinquished to the united states by any particular states pursuant to the recommendation of Congress of the 6 day of September last shall be disposed of for the common benefit of the united states and be settled and formed into distinct republican states which shall become members of the fœderal Union and have the same rights of Sovereignty freedom and independence as the other states

20. *RESOLUTION FOR EQUAL STATEHOOD FOR ACQUIRED TERRITORY, October 10, 1780, PCC No. 1, XXIX (unpaged), RG 360. 12⅞ x 8 in. 2 pages (excerpt illustrated).*

Victory and Independence

Although the independence of the United States had been recognized by France and the Netherlands when they entered into commercial treaties with the new republic in 1778 and 1782, it still had to be won by military victory and treaty from England. Only after Great Britain conceded the independence of her former colonies would the United States of America be admitted to the family of nations by most of the other governments of the world.

In October 1781 the Americans enjoyed the rare good fortune of having enough men, supplies, and naval power in the right place at the right time. The British had attempted to separate the southern from the northern States. After a costly victory at Guilford Court House Lord Cornwallis concentrated his forces at Yorktown, where he hoped to receive reinforcements and supplies from the British fleet. The timely arrival of Admiral de Grasse with the French fleet in Chesapeake Bay, however, dashed this hope. Meanwhile, General Washington had moved his own troops rapidly southward to join other forces near Yorktown. Helpless under the combined land siege and sea blockade, Cornwallis on October 17 agreed to capitulate. In his letter announcing the surrender, Washington wrote:

> I have the Honor to inform Congress, that a Reduction of the British Army under the Command of Lord Cornwallis, is most happily effected—The unremitting Ardor which actuated every Officer & Soldier in the combined Army on this Occasion, has principally led to this Important Event,—at an earlier period than my most sanguine Hopes had induced me to expect....
>
> On the 17th instant, a Letter was received from Lord Cornwallis, proposing a Meeting of Commissioners, to consult on Terms for the Surrender of the Ports

Head Quarters near York 19th Octr 1781.

Sir

I have the Honor to inform Congress, that
a Reduction of the British Army under the Command
of Lord Cornwallis, is most happily effected — The
unremitting Ardor which actuated every Officer & Soldier
in the combined Army on this Occasion, has princi-
pally led to this Important Event, — at an earlier
period than my most sanguine Hopes had induced me
to expect. — The singular Spirit of Emulation, which
animated the whole Army from the first Commence-
ment of our Operations, has filled my Mind with the
highest pleasure & Satisfaction — and had given me
the happiest presages of Success. —

On the 17th instant, a Letter was received from Lord Cornwallis, proposing a Meeting
of Commissioners, to consult on Terms for the Surrender
of the Posts of York & Gloucester — This Letter (the
first which had passed between us) opened a Correspondence, — a Copy of which I do myself the Honor to inclose,
that Correspondence was followed by the Definitive
Capitulation, which was agreed to, & signed on the 19th
Copy of which is also herewith transmitted — and which

21. *WASHINGTON'S ANNOUNCEMENT OF VICTORY AT YORKTOWN, October 19, 1781, PCC No. 152, X: 289-292, RG 360. 12½ x 8 in. Letter signed by Washington. 4 pages (page 1 illustrated). Endorsed: Entd Page 5/Letter from Genl Washington/October 19th 1781./read 24th/Reduction of ye British/Army under ye Command/of Lord Cornwallis./referred to Mr Randolph/Mr Boudinot/Mr Barnum/Mr Carroll*

Definitive treaty of peace with G Britain
3. Septr. 1783

45

Duplicate

In the Name of the most Holy and undivided Trinity:

It having pleased the Divine Providence to dispose the Hearts of the most Serene and most potent Prince George the Third, by the Grace of God, King of Great Britain, France and Ireland, Defender of the Faith, Duke of Brunswick and Luneburg, Arch Treasurer and Prince Elector of the Holy Roman Empire &c.a And of the United States of America, to forget all past Misunderstandings and Differences that have unhappily interrupted the good Correspondence and Friendship which they mutually wish to restore; and to establish such a beneficial and satisfactory Intercourse, between the two Countries upon the Ground of reciprocal Advantages and mutual Convenience as may promote and secure to both perpetual Peace & Harmony, and having for this desirable End already laid the Foundation of Peace and Reconciliation, by the Provisional Articles signed at Paris on the 30.th of November 1782, by the Commissioners empowered on each Part, which Articles were agreed to be inserted in and to constitute the Treaty of Peace proposed to be concluded between the Crown of Great Britain a

22. THE TREATY OF PARIS, *September 3, 1783, American Original (duplicate),* TS 104, RG 11. *14¾ x 9¾ in. 9 pages (pages 1 and 9 illustrated). Endorsed: Definitive treaty of peace with G. Britain/3 Sept. 1783*

Article 10.

The solemn Ratification of the present Treaty expedited in good and due Form shall be exchanged between the contracting Parties in the Space of six Months or sooner, if possible, to be computed from the Day of the Signature of the Present Treaty. In Witness whereof We the undersigned, their Ministers Plenipotentiary have in their Name and in Virtue of our full Powers, signed with our Hands the present Definitive Treaty, and caused the Seals of our Arms to be affixed thereto.

Done at Paris, this third Day of September In the Year of our Lord, one thousand, seven hundred and Eighty three.

D Hartley

John Adams.

B Franklin

John Jay

> of York & Gloucester—This Letter, (the first which had passed between us) opened a Correspondence,—a Copy of which I do myself the Honor to inclose, that Correspondence was followed by the Definitive Capitulation, which was agreed to, & signed on the 19th Copy of which is also herewith transmitted—and which I hope, will meet the Approbation of Congress.
>
> I should be wanting in the feelings of Gratitude, did I not mention on this Occasion, with the warmest Sense of Acknowlegments, the very chearfull & able Assistance, which I have received in the Course of our Operations, from his Excellency the Count de Rochambeau, and all his Officers of every Rank, in their respective Capacities.—Nothing could equal this Zeal of our Allies, but the emulating Spirit of the American Officers, whose Ardor would not suffer their Exertions to be exceeded. (Document 21.)

The surrender of Cornwallis and British military reverses elsewhere led to the fall of the British Ministry, and in March 1782 the way was open for peace negotiations. Although Congress appointed a five-man commission to go to Paris for this purpose, the principal peacemakers were Benjamin Franklin, John Adams, and John Jay. The other two appointees were Thomas Jefferson, who was unable to leave the United States, and Henry Laurens of South Carolina, who was not released from the Tower of London where he was a British prisoner in time to play a very significant role in the negotiations.

Preliminary articles of peace were signed in November 1782, and in September of the following yeaı the final treaty was signed at Paris. What is known as the American Revolution was in reality a world war involving not only England, the United States and its ally France, but also Spain and the Netherlands. On the same day that the Treaty of Paris (document 22) was signed between England and the United States, treaties were also signed between England and each of the other belligerents. The whole group of treaties formed the Peace of Paris of 1783.

The most important article of the Treaty of Paris was the first one:

> His Britannic Majesty acknowledges the said United States . . . to be free Sovereign & independant States. . . .

In addition, it provided that the territory of the United States should extend westward to the Mississippi River, southward to Florida, and northward to an ill-defined river and lakes boundary with Canada. Two other articles were of vital interest to Americans:

> Article 3d It is agreed that the People of the United States shall continue to enjoy unmolested the Right to take Fish of every Kind on the Grand Bank, and on all the other Banks of Newfoundland, also in the Gulph of Saint Lawrence and at all other Places in the Sea, where the Inhabitants of both Countries used at any time heretofore to fish. . . .
>
> Article 8th The Navigation of the River Mississippi . . . shall for ever remain free and open to the Subjects of Great Britain and the Citizens of the United States.

The treaty was signed by David Hartley for Great Britain and by Adams, Franklin, and Jay for the United States.

With the ratification of the Treaty of Paris by Congress on January 14, 1784, American independence was confirmed.

Skippet containing the seal of Great Britain affixed to the Treaty of Paris of 1783 (Exchange Copy).

"...a more perfect union..."

The United States as a Confederation

Bound together in the loose union provided by the Articles of Confederation, the United States struggled through seven years (1781-88) that have been called both a "critical period," because of the myriad problems which needed solution, and a "creative period," because of the number of problems which were at least partially solved. Many of the difficulties might have been experienced by any new nation in the process of establishing its identity among the nations of the world and its authority over its own people. But more and more American leaders came to blame every setback on the weakness of the confederation form of the government. The movement to strengthen the national government which culminated in the drafting of the Constitution of the United States was in actual fact a search for "a more perfect union."

Providing for the Public Domain

The United States in 1784 contained about a million square miles of land and slightly over three million people, not including Indians, whose numbers few tried to guess. To most citizens of the new Confederation, the future seemed as limitless and inviting as the vast empty wilderness awaiting settlement. It was therefore imperative that the Confederation Congress move quickly to enact a system of survey and government for the western land which now belonged to the Nation, since the States had surrendered their conflicting claims.

A committee composed of Thomas Jefferson, Jeremiah Townley Chase of Maryland, and David Howell of Rhode Island was given the task of proposing a "Plan for the Temporary Government of the Western Country" (document 23), which was presented to Congress on March 4, 1784. Reflecting Jefferson's ideas, it named and set specific boundaries for 10 States to be established northwest of the Ohio River, and provided that as settlers moved into each State, they should immediately set up their own government, patterning it after the constitution and laws of any one of the original 13 States. When the population reached 20,000 they were to hold a constitutional convention to create a permanent government and send a delegate to Congress. Once the State had a population equal to that of the smallest of the original 13 States, "such State shall be admitted by it's [*sic*] delegates into the Congress of the United States on an equal footing with the said original states. . . ."

The plan further provided:

> 4. That their respective governments shall be in republican forms, and shall admit no person to be a citizen who holds any hereditary title. 5. That after the year 1800 of the Christian æra, there shall be neither slavery nor involuntary servitude in any of the said states, otherwise than in punishment of crimes, whereof the party shall have been duly convicted to have been personally guilty.

Jefferson's proposal was finally adopted with some revisions and without the prohibitions against slavery and hereditary titles. Although no territorial governments were set up under it, this law attested to the good faith of the Confederation Congress in carrying out its 1780 pledge not to create from its public domain colonies which would forever remain subservient to the original 13 States of the Union.

Despite this measure and the Land Ordinance of 1785, which provided for survey of the public domain prior to sale, problems continued in the Northwest Territory. The British and their Indian allies refused to make way for American settlers. Squatters, impatient of ordinances passed by a distant Congress, moved onto the land and defended their illegal holdings against Indians and the Government forces alike. Meanwhile, pressure mounted to put the lands on sale. The Government needed revenue, Revolutionary veterans were eager to collect promised land bounties, and speculators formed into land companies and clamored for action.

Early in 1786, it was reported in Congress that the division of the "western Country" into States as provided by the Ordinance of 1784 was not "in any degree practicable." If the Ordinance remained in effect, many of the States, whose boundaries had been set with little knowledge of the topography of the area, would "not soon, if ever, have a sufficient number of Inhabitants to form a government; the consequence of which must be that they will continue without laws, and without order. . . ." At last, in July of 1787, the Confederation Congress repealed the Ordinance of 1784 and enacted "an Ordinance for the Government of the Territory of the United States, North-West of the River Ohio," more frequently referred to as the Northwest Ordinance of 1787 (document 24).

It provided for a territorial period during which the government should be under a governor, a secretary, and three judges, all to be appointed by Congress. Local control would begin gradually with the election of an assembly as population increased, and eventual statehood was still in prospect. Then in six articles it guaranteed certain rights, some of which were later guaranteed by the Constitution and the Bill of Rights. Among these were religious freedom, the benefit of the writ of habeas corpus, and trial by jury. Education was encouraged and it was declared:

> There shall be neither slavery nor involuntary servitude in the said territory, otherwise than in punishment of crimes whereof the party shall have been duly convicted. . . .

Other Problems of the Confederation

Having shown creative statesmanship of a high order in its provision for the distribution and government of the public domain, the Congress of the Confederation was unable to deal with some of the other problems of the new nation. Although Congress alone had power to coin money, any state could issue paper bills; when several did so, businessmen complained that the currency was in chaos. Congress could only request financial support from the States; there was no way it could cœrce them.

Little could be done about the States which moved slowly to fulfill the terms of the Treaty of Paris in regard to the property of Americans who had remained loyal to England during the Revolution, or to debts owed by Americans to British creditors. It was partially in retaliation that the British continued to occupy seven forts in the Northwest Territory which had been ceded to the United States in 1783.

In other foreign affairs, Spain refused to accept the Florida boundary and the provision for free navigation of the Mississippi River provided for in the Treaty of Paris, and although Prussia concluded a commercial treaty with the United States in 1785, many European nations expected the United States to disintegrate as a nation.

Finally, the unanimous vote of the States required to amend the Articles was unobtainable.

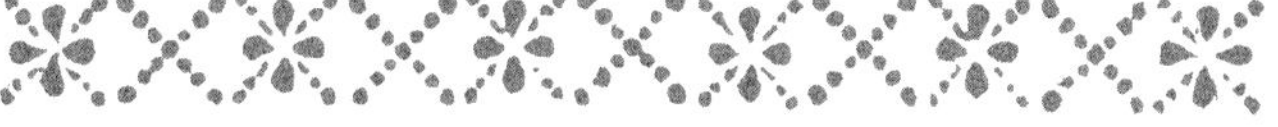

Provided that both the temporary & permanent governments be establish-ed on these principles as ~~their basis~~ 1. that they shall for ever remain a part of the United states of America. 2. that in their persons, property & territory they shall be subject to the government of the United states in Congress assembled, and to the Articles of confederation in all those cases in which the original states shall be so subject. 3. that they shall be subject to pay a part of the federal debts contracted or to be contracted to be apportioned on them by Congress according to the same common rule and measure by which apportionments thereof shall be made on the other states. 4. That their respective governments shall be in republi-can forms, and shall admit no person to be a citizen who holds any here-ditary title. 5. That after the year 1800 of the Christian aera, there shall be neither slavery nor involuntary servitude in any of the said states, otherwise than in punishment of crimes, whereof the party shall have been duly con-victed to have been personally guilty.

That whensoever any of the sd states shall have, of free inhabitants, as many as shall then be in any one the least numerous of the thirteen original states, such state shall be admitted by it's delegates into the Congress of the United states, on an equal footing with the said original states: after which the assent of ~~two thirds of the~~ United states in Congress assem-bled shall be requisite in all those cases, wherein by the Confederation the assent of nine states is now required. provided the consent of nine states to such admission may be obtained according to the eleventh of the articles of Confederation. Until such admission by their delegates into Congress, any of the said states, after the establishment of their temporary government, shall have authority to keep a sitting member in Congress, with a right of debating, but not of voting.

23. A PLAN FOR THE GOVERNMENT OF THE WESTERN COUNTRY, March 1, 1784, PCC No. 30, I: 49-51, RG 360. Pages 49, 50. 8⅞ x 7 in. Page 51 8¾ x 7⅜ in. 3 pages (pages 50 and 51 illustrated). *In the hand of Thomas Jefferson. 3 pages (pp. 2 and 3 illustrated). Endorsed:* Report Mr Jefferson/Mr Chase/Mr Howell/Temporary governmt/of western Country/Delivered 1 March 1784/Entd–Read./March 3./Monday next assigned for/the consideration of this report/March 7. 1784/recommitted

51

That the territory Northward of the 45th degree, that is to say of the completion of 45° from the Equator, & ~~Westward of Lakes Superior~~ extending to the Lake of the Woods, shall be called **Sylvania**:

That of the territory under the 45th & 44th degrees that which lies Westward of Lake Michigan shall be called **Michigania**, and that which is Eastward thereof ~~and nearly surrounded~~ within the peninsul formed by the lakes & waters of Michigan, Huron, St. Clair and Erie, shall be called **Cherronesus**, and shall include any part of the peninsul which may extend above the 45th degree.

Of the territory under the 43d & 42d degrees, that to the Westward thro' which the Assenisipi or Rock river runs shall be called **Assenisipia**, and that to the Eastward in which are the fountains of the Muskingum, the two Miamis of Ohio, the Wabash, the Illinois, the Miami of the lake and Sandusky rivers, shall be called **Metropotamia**.

Of the territory which lies under the 41st & 40th degrees, the Western, thro which the river Illinois runs, shall be called **Illinoia**; that next adjoining to the Eastward **Saratoga**, and that between this last & Pennsylvania & extending from the Ohio to Lake Erie, shall be called **Washington**.

Of the territory which lies under the 39th & 38th degrees to which shall be added so much of the point of land within the fork of the Ohio & Missisipi as lies under the 37th degree, that to the Westward within & adjacent to which are the confluences of the rivers Wabash, Shawanee, Tanisee, Ohio, Illinois, Missisipi & Missouri, shall be called **Polypotamia**, and that to the Eastward farther up the Ohio, otherwise called the Pelisipi shall be called **Pelisipia**.

That the preceding articles shall be formed into a Charter of Compact shall be duly executed by the President of the U.S. in Congress assembled under his hand & the seal of the United States, shall be promulgated, and shall stand as fundamental constitutions between the thirteen original states, & those now newly described unalterable but by the joint consent of the U.S. in Congress assembled and of the particular state within which such alteration is proposed to be made.

An ORDINANCE for the GOVERNMENT of the TERRITORY of the UNITED STATES, North-West of the RIVER OHIO.

BE IT ORDAINED by the United States in Congress assembled, That the said territory, for the purposes of temporary government, be one district; subject, however, to be divided into two districts, as future circumstances may, in the opinion of Congress, make it expedient.

Be it ordained by the authority aforesaid, That the estates both of resident and non-resident proprietors in the said territory, dying intestate, shall descend to, and be distributed among their children, and the descendants of a deceased child in equal parts; the descendants of a deceased child or grand-child, to take the share of their deceased parent in equal parts among them: And where there shall be no children or descendants, then in equal parts to the next of kin, in equal degree; and among collaterals, the children of a deceased brother or sister of the intestate, shall have in equal parts among them their deceased parents share; and there shall in no case be a distinction between kindred of the whole and half blood; saving in all cases to the widow of the intestate, her third part of the real estate for life, and one third part of the personal estate; and this law relative to descents and dower, shall remain in full force until altered by the legislature of the district. ——— And until the governor and judges shall adopt laws as herein after mentioned, estates in the said territory may be devised or bequeathed by wills in writing, signed and sealed by him or her, in whom the estate may be, (being of full age) and attested by three witnesses; — and real estates may be conveyed by lease and release, or bargain and sale, signed, sealed, and delivered by the person being of full age, in whom the estate may be, and attested by two witnesses, provided such wills be duly proved, and such conveyances be acknowledged, or the execution thereof duly proved, and be recorded within one year after proper magistrates, courts, and registers shall be appointed for that purpose; and personal property may be transferred by delivery, saving, however, to the French and Canadian inhabitants, and other settlers of the Kaskaskies, Saint Vincent's, and the neighbouring villages, who have heretofore professed themselves citizens of Virginia, their laws and customs now in force among them, relative to the descent and conveyance of property.

Be it ordained by the authority aforesaid, That there shall be appointed from time to time, by Congress, a governor, whose commission shall continue in force for the term of three years, unless sooner revoked by Congress; he shall reside in the district, and have a freehold estate therein, in one thousand acres of land, while in the exercise of his office.

There shall be appointed from time to time, by Congress, a secretary, whose commission shall continue in force for four years, unless sooner revoked, he shall reside in the district, and have a freehold estate therein, in five hundred acres of land, while in the exercise of his office; it shall be his duty to keep and preserve the acts and laws passed by the legislature, and the public records of the district, and the proceedings of the governor in his executive department; and transmit authentic copies of such acts and proceedings, every six months, to the secretary of Congress: There shall also be appointed a court to consist of three judges, any two of whom to form a court, who shall have a common law jurisdiction, and reside in the district, and have each therein a freehold estate in five hundred acres of land, while in the exercise of their offices; and their commissions shall continue in force during good behaviour.

The governor and judges, or a majority of them, shall adopt and publish in the district, such laws of the original states, criminal and civil, as may be necessary, and best suited to the circumstances of the district, and report them to Congress, from time to time, which laws shall be in force in the district until the organization of the general assembly therein, unless disapproved of by Congress; but afterwards the legislature shall have authority to alter them as they shall think fit.

The governor for the time being, shall be commander in chief of the militia, appoint and commission all officers in the same, below the rank of general officers; all general officers shall be appointed and commissioned by Congress.

Previous to the organization of the general assembly, the governor shall appoint such magistrates and other civil officers, in each county or township, as he shall find necessary for the preservation of the peace and good order in the same: After the general assembly shall be organized, the powers and duties of magistrates and other civil officers shall be regulated and defined by the said assembly; but all magistrates and other civil officers, not herein otherwise directed, shall, during the continuance of this temporary government, be appointed by the governor.

For the prevention of crimes and injuries, the laws to be adopted or made shall have force in all parts of the district, and for the execution of process, criminal and civil, the governor shall make proper divisions thereof—and he shall proceed from time to time, as circumstances may require, to lay out the parts of the district in which the Indian titles shall have been extinguished, into counties and townships, subject, however, to such alterations as may thereafter be made by the legislature.

So soon as there shall be five thousand free male inhabitants, of full age, in the district, upon giving proof thereof to the governor, they shall receive authority, with time and place, to elect representatives from their counties or townships, to represent them in the general assembly; provided that for every five hundred free male inhabitants there shall be one representative, and so on progressively with the number of free male inhabitants, shall the right of representation increase, until the number of representatives shall amount to twenty-five, after which the number and proportion of representatives shall be regulated by the legislature; provided that no person be eligible or qualified to act as a representative, unless he shall have been a citizen of one of the United States three years and be a resident in the district, or unless he shall have resided in the district three years, and in either case shall likewise hold in his own right, in fee simple, two hundred acres of land within the same:---Provided also, that a freehold in fifty acres of land in the district, having been a citizen of one of the states, and being resident in the district; or the like freehold and two years residence in the district shall be necessary to qualify a man as an elector of a representative.

The representatives thus elected, shall serve for the term of two years, and in case of the death of a representative, or removal from office, the governor shall issue a writ to the county or township for which he was a member, to elect another in his stead, to serve for the residue of the term.

The general assembly, or legislature, shall consist of the governor, legislative council, and a house of representatives. The legislative council shall consist of five members, to continue in office five years, unless sooner removed by Congress, any three of whom to be a quorum, and the members of the council shall be nominated and appointed in the following manner, to wit: As soon as representatives shall be elected, the governor shall appoint a time and place for them to meet together, and, when met, they shall nominate ten persons, residents in the district, and each possessed of a freehold in five hundred acres of land, and return their names to Congress; five of whom Congress shall appoint and commission to serve as aforesaid; and whenever a vacancy shall happen in the council, by death or removal from office, the house of representatives shall nominate two persons, qualified as aforesaid, for each vacancy, and return their names to Congress; one of whom Congress shall appoint and commission for the residue of the term; and every five years, four months at least before the expiration of the time of service of the members of council, the said house shall nominate ten persons, qualified as aforesaid, and return their names to Congress, five of whom Congress shall appoint and commission to serve as members of the council five years, unless sooner removed. And the governor, legislative council, and house of re-

24. *THE ORDINANCE OF 1787, July 13, 1787, PCC No. 59, I: 229-230, RG 360. 12¾ x 8 in. Broadsheet attested by the signature of Charles Thomson. 2 pages.*

preſentatives, ſhall have authority to make laws in all caſes for the good government of the diſtrict, not repugnant to the principles and articles in this ordinance eſtabliſhed and declared. And all bills having paſſed by a majority in the houſe, and by a majority in the council, ſhall be referred to the governor for his aſſent; but no bill or legiſlative act whatever, ſhall be of any force without his aſſent. The governor ſhall have power to convene, prorogue and diſſolve the general aſſembly, when in his opinion it ſhall be expedient.

The governor, judges, legiſlative council, ſecretary, and ſuch other officers as Congreſs ſhall appoint in the diſtrict, ſhall take an oath or affirmation of fidelity, and of office, the governor before the preſident of Congreſs, and all other officers before the governor. As ſoon as a legiſlature ſhall be formed in the diſtrict, the council and houſe, aſſembled in one room, ſhall have authority by joint ballot to elect a delegate to Congreſs, who ſhall have a ſeat in Congreſs, with a right of debating, but not of voting, during this temporary government.

And for extending the fundamental principles of civil and religious liberty, which form the baſis whereon theſe republics, their laws and conſtitutions are erected; to fix and eſtabliſh thoſe principles as the baſis of all laws, conſtitutions and governments, which for ever hereafter ſhall be formed in the ſaid territory;---to provide alſo for the eſtabliſhment of ſtates, and permanent government therein, and for their admiſſion to a ſhare in the federal councils on an equal footing with the original ſtates, at as early periods as may be conſiſtent with the general intereſt:

It is hereby ordained and declared by the authority aforeſaid, That the following articles ſhall be conſidered as articles of compact between the original ſtates and the people and ſtates in the ſaid territory, and forever remain unalterable, unleſs by common conſent, to wit:

Article the Firſt. No perſon, demeaning himſelf in a peaceable and orderly manner, ſhall ever be moleſted on account of his mode of worſhip or religious ſentiments in the ſaid territory.

Article the Second. The inhabitants of the ſaid territory ſhall always be entitled to the benefits of the writ of habeas corpus, and of the trial by jury; of a proportionate repreſentation of the people in the legiſlature, and of judicial proceedings according to the courſe of the common law; all perſons ſhall be bailable unleſs for capital offences, where the proof ſhall be evident, or the preſumption great; all fines ſhall be moderate, and no cruel or unuſual puniſhments ſhall be inflicted; no man ſhall be deprived of his liberty or property but by the judgment of his peers, or the law of the land; and ſhould the public exigencies make it neceſſary for the common preſervation to take any perſon's property, or to demand his particular ſervices, full compenſation ſhall be made for the ſame; — and in the juſt preſervation of rights and property it is underſtood and declared, that no law ought ever to be made, or have force in the ſaid territory, that ſhall in any manner whatever interfere with, or affect private contracts or engagements, bona fide and without fraud previouſly formed.

Article the Third. Religion, morality and knowledge, being neceſſary to good government and the happineſs of mankind, ſchools and the means of education ſhall forever be encouraged. The utmoſt good faith ſhall always be obſerved towards the Indians; their lands and property ſhall never be taken from them without their conſent; and in their property, rights and liberty, they never ſhall be invaded or diſturbed, unleſs in juſt and lawful wars authoriſed by Congreſs; but laws founded in juſtice and humanity ſhall from time to time be made, for preventing wrongs being done to them, and for preſerving peace and friendſhip with them..

Article the Fourth. The ſaid territory, and the ſtates which may be formed therein, ſhall forever remain a part of this confederacy of the United States of America, ſubject to the articles of confederation, and to ſuch alterations therein as ſhall be conſtitutionally made; and to all the acts and ordinances of the United ſtates in Congreſs aſſembled, conformable thereto. The inhabitants and ſettlers in the ſaid territory, ſhall be ſubject to pay a part of the federal debts contracted or to be contracted, and a proportional part of the expences of government, to be apportioned on them by Congreſs, according to the ſame common rule and meaſure by which apportionments thereof ſhall be made on the other ſtates; and the taxes for paying their proportion, ſhall be laid and levied by the authority and direction of the legiſlatures of the diſtrict or diſtricts or new ſtates, as in the original ſtates, within the time agreed upon by the United States in Congreſs aſſembled. The legiſlatures of thoſe diſtricts, or new ſtates, ſhall never interfere with the primary diſpoſal of the ſoil by the United States in Congreſs aſſembled, nor with any regulations Congreſs may find neceſſary for ſecuring the title in ſuch ſoil to the bona fide purchaſers. No tax ſhall be impoſed on lands the property of the United States; and in no caſe ſhall non-reſident proprietors be taxed higher than reſidents. The navigable waters leading into the Miſſiſippi and St. Lawrence, and the carrying places between the ſame ſhall be common highways, and forever free, as well to the inhabitants of the ſaid territory, as to the citizens of the United States, and thoſe of any other ſtates that may be admitted into the confederacy, without any tax, impoſt or duty therefor.

Articls the Fifth. There ſhall be formed in the ſaid territory, not leſs than three nor more than five ſtates; and the boundaries of the ſtates, as ſoon as Virginia ſhall alter her act of ceſſion and conſent to the ſame, ſhall become fixed and eſtabliſhed as follows, to wit: The weſtern ſtate in the ſaid territory, ſhall be bounded by the Miſſiſippi, the Ohio and Wabaſh rivers; a direct line drawn from the Wabaſh and Poſt Vincent's due north to the territorial line between the United States and Canada, and by the ſaid territorial line to the lake of the Woods and Miſſiſippi. The middle ſtate ſhall be bounded by the ſaid direct line, the Wabaſh from Poſt Vincent's to the Ohio; by the Ohio, by a direct line drawn due north from the mouth of the Great Miami to the ſaid territorial line, and by the ſaid territorial line. The eaſtern ſtate ſhall be bounded by the laſt mentioned direct line, the Ohio, Pennſylvania, and the ſaid territorial line; Provided however, and it is further underſtood and declared, that the boundaries of theſe three ſtates, ſhall be ſubject ſo far to be altered, that if Congreſs ſhall hereafter find it expedient, they ſhall have authority to form one or two ſtates in that part of the ſaid territory which lies north of an eaſt and weſt line drawn through the ſoutherly bend or extreme of lake Michigan: and whenever any of the ſaid ſtates ſhall have ſixty thouſand free inhabitants therein, ſuch ſtate ſhall be admitted by its delegates into the Congreſs of the United ſtates, on an equal footing with the original ſtates in all reſpects whatever; and ſhall be at liberty to form a permanent conſtitution and ſtate government: Provided the conſtitution and government ſo to be formed, ſhall be republican, and in conformity to the principles contained in theſe articles; and ſo far as it can be conſiſtent with the general intereſt of the confederacy, ſuch admiſſion ſhall be allowed at an earlier period, and when there may be a leſs number of free inhabitants in the ſtate than ſixty thouſand.

Article the Sixth. There ſhall be neither ſlavery nor involuntary ſervitude in the ſaid territory, otherwiſe than in puniſhment of crimes whereof the party ſhall have been duly convicted: Provided always, that any perſon eſcaping into the ſame, from whom labor or ſervice is lawfully claimed in any one of the original ſtates, ſuch fugitive may be lawfully reclaimed and conveyed to the perſon claiming his or her labor or ſervice as aforeſaid.

Be it ordained by the authority aforeſaid, That the reſolutions of the 23d of April, 1784, relative to the ſubject of this ordinance, be, and the ſame are hereby repealed and declared null and void.

DONE by the UNITED STATES in CONGRESS aſſembled, the 13th day of July, in the year of our Lord 1787, and of their ſovereignty and independence the 12th.

Chas Thomson Secy

Movement to Strengthen the National Government

One of the most vexing problems of the Confederation arose from the inability of the Confederation Congress to regulate interstate commerce. Where there was a disagreement between two States about trade, they had to negotiate the matter much as two nations might have done.

When Virginia and Maryland had successfully settled their dispute over navigation and commerce on Chesapeake Bay through an interstate agreement at a meeting at Mt. Vernon, the Virginia Legislature in 1786 proposed a convention to consider commercial regulations among all the States. The response was favorable and a meeting of State commissioners was held at Annapolis in September 1786. At this meeting delegates from only five States appeared, although nine had named commissioners. Nevertheless, in an unanimous report (document 25), the Annapolis Convention recommended "To the Honorable, the Legislatures of Virginia, Delaware[,] Pennsylvania, New Jersey, and New York that

> ... it may essentially tend to advance the interests of the union, if the States, by whom they have been respectively delegated. would themselves concur, and use their endeavours to procure the concurrence of the other States. in the appointment of Commissioners, to meet at Philadelphia on the second Monday in May next. to take into consideration the situation of the United States, to devise such further provisions as shall appear to them necessary to render the constitution of the Fœderal Government adequate to the exigencies of the Union; and to report such an Act for that purpose to the United States in Congress Assembled. as when agreed to, by them. and afterwards confirmed by the Legislatures of every State. will effectually provide for the same.

Congress received the report of the Annapolis Convention coldly and took no action on the recommendation of the commissioners. Virginia, however, acted favorably on the proposal; it selected delegates and asked the concurrence of the other States. By February 1787 several States had concurred with Virginia. Their action helped to change Congressional sentiment, as did the influence of Thomas Jefferson's friend, James Madison, and George Washington's young former aide-de-camp, Alexander Hamilton of New York. Both had served as delegates in the Confederation Congress, and believed that the national government must be given more power if the nation was to survive.

On February 21, 1787, the Confederation Congress passed a resolution which, while making no mention of the Annapolis Convention, called for a convention of delegates of the States in Philadelphia in May:

> Whereas there is provision in the Articles of Confederation & perpetual Union for making alterations therein by the Assent of a Congress of the United States and of the legislatures of the several States; And whereas experience hath evinced that there are defects in the present Confederation, as a mean to remedy which several of the States and particularly the State of New York by express instructions to their delegates in Congress have suggested a convention for the purposes expressed in the following resolution and such Convention appearing to be the most probable mean of establishing in these states a firm national government
>
> Resolved that in the Opinion of Congress it is expedient that on the second Monday in May next a Convention of delegates who shall have been appointed by the several States be held at Philadelphia for the sole and express purpose of revising the Articles of Confederation and reporting to Congress and the several legislatures such alterations and provisions therein as shall when agreed to in Congress and confirmed by the States render the federal constitution adequate to the exigencies of Government & the preservation of the Union. (Document 26.)

The Constitutional Convention

The convention that was called to amend the Articles of Confederation but that was actually to write the Constitution of the United States was often called the "Fœderal Convention" in contemporary newspapers. After it convened in the State House in Philadelphia on May 14, 1787, delegates continued to arrive slowly, and by the end of July 12 States were represented. Rhode Island refused to participate.

Many of the delegates had served in the Confederation Congress. Benjamin Franklin was there, at 81 the oldest member of the Convention. Roger Sherman, the only man who signed the Declaration of Independence, the Articles of Confederation, and later the Constitution, was a delegate from Connecticut. John Dickinson, who had tried to push through a stronger constitution in 1776 when he offered his draft of the Articles of Confederation, represented Delaware. And George Washington was elected President of the Convention.

on the subject, they have been induced to think, that the power of regulating trade is of such comprehensive extent, and will enter so far into the general System of the federal government, that to give it efficacy, and to obviate questions and doubts concerning its precise nature and limits, may require a correspondent adjustment of other parts of the Federal System.

That there are important defects in the system of the Federal Government is acknowledged by the Acts of all those States, which have concurred in the present Meeting; That the defects, upon a closer examination, may be found greater and more numerous, than even these acts imply, is at least so far probable, from the embarrassments which characterise the present State of our national affairs, foreign and domestic, as may reasonably be supposed to merit a deliberate and candid discussion, in some mode, which will unite the Sentiments and Councils of all the States. In the choice of the mode, your Commissioners are of opinion, that a Convention of Deputies from the different States, for the special and sole purpose of entering into this investigation, and digesting a plan for supplying such defects as may be discovered to exist, will be entitled to a preference from considerations, which will occur, without being particularised.

Your Commissioners decline an enumeration of those national circumstances on which their opinion respecting the propriety of a future Convention with more enlarged powers, is founded; as it would be an useless intrusion of facts and observations, most of which have been frequently the subject of public discussion, and none of which can have escaped the penetration of those to whom they would in this instance be addressed. They are however of a nature so serious, as, in the view of your Commissioners to render the situation of the United States delicate and critical, calling for an exertion of the united virtue and wisdom of all the members of the Confederacy.

Under this impression, Your Commissioners, with the most respectful deference, beg leave to suggest their unanimous conviction, that it may essentially tend to advance the interests of the union, if the States, by whom they have been respectively delegated, would themselves concur, and use their endeavours to procure the concurrence of the other States, in the appointment of Commissioners, to meet at Philadelphia on the second Monday in May next, to take into consideration the situation of the United States, to devise such further provisions as shall appear to them necessary

25. *REPORT OF THE ANNAPOLIS CONVENTION, September 14, 1786, Papers of the Constitutional Convention, RG 360. 15½ x 10 in. Signed by delegates from five states. 5 pages (pages 4 and 5 illustrated). Endorsed: Report of the Commissioners at/Annapolis, September 14. 1786./ /Report of the Commissione[r]s/of N York N Jersey/Pensylvania Delaware/an[d] Virginia at/Annapolis/N° 51*

necessary to render the constitution of the Foederal Government adequate to the exigencies of the Union; and to report such an Act for that purpose to the United States in Congress Assembled. as when agreed to, by them. and afterwards confirmed by the Legislatures of every State. will effectually provide for the same.

Though your Commissioners could not with propriety address these observations and sentiments to any but the States they have the honor to Represent. they have nevertheless concluded from motives of respect. to transmit Copies of this Report to the United States in Congress assembled. and to the executives of the other States.

By order of the Commissioners

Dated at Annapolis
September 14th. 1786

Resolved that the Chairman sign the aforegoing Report in behalf of the Commissioners

Then adjourned without day—

Egbt. Benson
Alexander Hamilton — New York

Abra: Clark
Wm Chs Houston
Js. Schureman — New Jersey

Tench Coxe — Pennsylvania

Geo: Read
John Dickinson
Richard Bassett — Delaware

Edmund Randolph.
Js. Madison Jr.
St. George Tucker — Virginia

(Continuation of Document 25)

Whereas there is provision in the Articles of Confederation & Perpetual Union for making alterations therein by the Assent of a Congress of the United States and of the Legislatures of the several States; And whereas experience hath evinced that there are defects in the present Confederation, as a mean to remedy which several of the States and particularly the State of New York by express instructions to their delegates in Congress have suggested a convention for the purposes expressed in the following resolution and such Convention appearing to be the most probable mean of establishing in these States a firm national government

Resolved that in the opinion of Congress it is expedient that on the second Monday in May next a Convention of delegates who shall have been appointed by the several States be held at Philadelphia for the sole and express purpose of revising the Articles of Confederation and reporting to Congress and the several legislatures such alterations and

1787 Feby 21

provisions therein as shall when agreed to in Congress and confirmed by the States render the federal constitution adequate to the exigencies of Government & the preservation of the Union

26. RESOLUTION CALLING FOR PHILADELPHIA CONVENTION, *February 21, 1787, PCC No. 1, XXXVIII (unpaged), RG 360. 12½ x 7¾ in. 2 pages.*

Two familiar names were not on the list of members: John Adams was representing his country in London, and Thomas Jefferson had replaced Franklin as the American Minister to France. But both were very interested in the outcome.

The Great Compromise

By May 29, the Convention had adopted rules of order and procedure, and agreed to keep its proceedings secret.

Edmund Randolph of Virginia then submitted for the consideration of the Convention the Virginia Plan. This proposal, consisting of 15 suggestions for the amendment of the Articles of Confederation, had been prepared by the Virginia delegation under the thoughtful leadership of James Madison.

For the next two weeks the Convention, meeting as a Committee of the Whole, discussed and amended this plan. When the Committee reported to the Convention the amended plan in the form of 19 resolutions, it was obvious that, rather than amending the Articles, the Convention would draft an entirely new frame of government. Although it underwent a number of modifications, the Virginia Plan formed the basis of the finished Constitution. Among the resolutions proposed by the Committee were the following:

> 1. Resolved that it is the opinion of this Committee that a national government ought to be established consisting of a Supreme Legislative, Judiciary, and Executive.
>
> 2 Resolved that the national Legislature ought to consist of Two Branches.
>
> 3 Resolved that the Members of the first branch of the national Legislature ought to be elected by the People of the several States. . . .
>
> 4 Resolved. that the Members of the Second Branch of the national Legislature ought to be chosen by the individual Legislatures. . . .
>
> 9 Resolved. that a national Executive be instituted to consist of a Single Person. . . .
>
> 11 Resolved. that a national Judiciary be established to consist of One supreme Tribunal. . . .
>
> 12 Resolved. That the national Legislature be empowered to appoint inferior Tribunals. (Document 27.)

Members of both "branches" of the "national Legislature" were "to be paid out of the National Treasury" instead of by the States, an important step in making a member of Congress part of the National rather than the State Government.

To delegates from the small States there were features of the revised Virginia Plan which were very disturbing, and, their numbers augmented by some late arrivals, they countered with their own plan on June 15. William Paterson of New Jersey laid before the convention an alternate proposal which more nearly approached the revision of the Articles of Confederation which the delegates had been instructed to undertake. It provided for a single-house Congress with equal representation for all states. Although the New Jersey Plan as a whole was defeated by a vote of 7 States to 3 on June 19, in the clause-by-clause consideration of the Virginia Plan, the small States picked up enough support on July 2 to deadlock the convention, 5 to 5, on the proposal to base representation in both houses of Congress on population.

For two discouraging weeks in the sweltering heat of July in Philadelphia, the delegates struggled to find a way out of the impasse. John Dickinson had already suggested that one house of the "legislative branch" could represent population and the other the States. Finally, on July 16 a group of resolutions dealing with representation was adopted (document 28), and the deadlock was broken. During the remainder of the long summer other matters had to be thrashed out among delegates with opposing views, but this was the Great Compromise without which the Constitution might not have been adopted: an upper house in which the States were equally represented, a lower house with representation based upon population as enumerated in a decennial census, and all money bills originating in the lower house.

On August 6 the Committee of Detail presented to the Convention the first printed draft of the Constitution (document 29). The preamble began, "We the People of the States of New-Hampshire, Massachusetts . . . and Georgia." The Committee of Style and Arrangement, which reported on September 12, made one striking change. The preamble read:

> We, the People of the United States, in order to form a more perfect union, to establish justice, insure domestic tranquility, provide for the common defence, promote the general welfare, and secure the blessings of liberty to ourselves and our posterity, do ordain and establish this Constitution for the United States of America.

With a few alterations the September 12 version was ordered to be engrossed on September 15. On the following Monday, September 17, one additional change was made in the engrossed copy and the Constitution adopted "by the Unanimous Consent of the States present" was ready to be signed.

State of the resolutions submitted to the consideration of the House by the honorable Mr Randolph, as altered, amended, and agreed to in a Committee of the whole House.

1. Resolved that it is the opinion of this Committee that a national government ought to be established consisting of a Supreme Legislative, Judiciary, and Executive.

2 Resolved that the national legislature ought to consist of Two Branches.

3 Resolved that the members of the first branch of the national Legislature ought to be elected by
the People of the several States
for the term of Three years.
to receive fixed stipends, by which they may be compensated for the devotion of their time to public service
to be paid out of the National Treasury.
to be ineligible to any Office established by a particular State or under the authority of the United States (except those peculiarly belonging to the functions of the first branch) during the term of service, and under the national government for the space of one year after it's expiration.

4 Resolved. that the members of the second Branch of the national Legislature ought to be chosen by
the individual Legislatures.
to be of the age of thirty years at least.
to hold their offices for a term sufficient to ensure their independency, namely
seven years.
to receive fixed stipends, by which they may be compensated for the devotion of their time to public service - to be paid out of the National Treasury
to be ineligible to any Office established by a particular State, or under the authority of the United States (except those peculiarly belonging to the functions of the second branch) during the term of service, and under the national government, for the space of One year after it's expiration.

27. THE VIRGINIA PLAN AS AMENDED IN THE PHILADELPHIA CONVENTION, *June 13, 1787, Papers of the Constitutional Convention, RG 360. 12⅞ x 8 in. 4 pages (pages 1 and 2 illustrated). Endorsed (in Timothy Pickering's hand): Received. this sheet from the President of the United/States, with the journals of the General Convention,/March 19th 1796. Timothy Pickering/ Secy of State./ /No 2/State of the Resolutions/submit-/ted by Mr Randolph to the Con-/sideration of the House, as altered, amended & agreed/to in a Committee of the whole/House./Received from the President/of the U. States, march/19. 1796. by/Timothy Pickering/Secy of State*

5. Resolved that each branch ought to possess the right of originating acts

6. Resolved. that the national Legislature ought to be empowered
to enjoy the legislative rights vested in Congress by the confederation – and moreover
to legislate in all cases to which the separate States are incompetent: or in which the harmony of the United States may be interrupted by the exercise of individual legislation.
to negative all laws passed by the several States contravening, in the opinion of the national legislature, the articles of union, or any treaties subsisting under the authority of the union.

7. Resolved. that the right of suffrage in the first branch of the national legislature ought not to be according to the rule established in the articles of confederation: but according to some equitable ratio of representation – namely.
p. 20.
in proportion to the whole number of white and other free citizens and inhabitants of every age, sex, and condition including those bound to servitude for a term of years, and three fifths of all other persons not comprehended in the foregoing description, except Indians, not paying taxes in each State.

8 Resolved. that the right of suffrage in the second branch of the national legislature ought to be according to the rule established for the first
p. 21

9 Resolved. that a national Executive be instituted to consist of a Single Person.
to be chosen by the National legislature.
for the term of Seven years.
with power to carry into execution the national laws.
to appoint to Offices in cases not otherwise provided for
to be ineligible a second time, and
to be removable on impeachment and conviction of mal practice or neglect of duty.
to receive a fixed stipend, by which he may be compensated for the devotion of his time to public service
to be paid out of the national Treasury

(Continuation of Document 27)

54 Journal of the federal Convention Monday July 16. 1787.

The question being taken on the whole of the report from the grand Committee as amended

81 it passed in the affirmative

and is as follows, namely.

Resolved — That in the original formation of the Legislature of the United States the first Branch thereof shall consist of Sixty five members — of which number

New Hampshire shall send — Three
Massachusetts ———— Eight
Rhode Island ———— One
Connecticut ———— Five
New York ———— Six
New Jersey ———— four
Pennsylvania ———— Eight
Delaware ———— One
Maryland ———— Six
Virginia ———— Ten
North Carolina ———— Five
South Carolina ———— Five
Georgia ———— Three.

But as the present situation of the States may probably alter in the number of their inhabitants the Legislature of the United States shall be authorised from time to time to apportion the number of representatives: and in case any of the States shall hereafter be divided, or enlarged by addition of territory, or any two or more States united, or any new States created within the limits of the United States the Legislature of the United States shall possess authority to regulate the number of representatives: ~~and~~ in ~~case~~ any of the foregoing cases upon the principle of their number of inhabitants, according

28. *THE GREAT COMPROMISE, July 16, 1787, Journal of the Federal Convention, pp. 54-55, Papers of the Constitutional Convention, RG 360. 16 x 12¾ in. In the hand of William Jackson, Secretary of the Convention. 2 pages.*

Journal of the federal Convention Monday July 16th 1787.

to the provisions hereafter mentioned, namely,

Provided always that representation ought to be proportioned according to direct Taxation; and in order to ascertain the alteration in the direct Taxation, which may be required from time to time by the changes in the relative circumstances of the States - Resolved that a Census be taken within six years from the first meeting of the Legislature of the United States, and once within the term of every Ten years afterwards, of all the inhabitants of the United States in the manner and according to the ratio recommended by Congress in their resolution of April 18th 1783 - and that the Legislature of the United States shall proportion the direct Taxation accordingly.

Resolved That all Bills for raising or appropriating money, and for fixing the salaries of the Officers of the Government of the United States shall originate in the first Branch of the Legislature of the United States, and shall not be altered or amended by the second Branch - and that no money shall be drawn from the Public Treasury but in pursuance of appropriations to be originated by the first Branch.

Resolved That in the second Branch of the Legislature of the United States each State shall have an equal vote.

It was moved and seconded to agree to the first clause of the sixth resolution reported from the Committee of the whole House namely

"That the national Legislature ought to possess the legislative rights vested in Congress by the confederation"

which passed unanimously in the affirmative

It was moved and seconded to commit the second clause of the sixth resolution reported from the Committee of the whole House

which passed in the negative

And then the House adjourned till to-morrow at 11 o'Clock A.M.

(Continuation of Document 28)

WE the People of the States of New-Hampſhire, Maſſachuſetts, Rhode-Iſland and Providence Plantations, Connecticut, New-York, New-Jerſey, Pennſylvania, Delaware, Maryland, Virginia, North-Carolina, South-Carolina, and Georgia, do ordain, declare and eſtabliſh the following Conſtitution for the Government of Ourſelves and our Poſterity.

ARTICLE I.

The ſtile of this Government ſhall be, "The United States of America."

II.

The Government ſhall conſiſt of ſupreme legiſlative, executive and judicial powers.

III.

The legiſlative power ſhall be veſted in a Congreſs, to conſiſt of two ſeparate and diſtinct bodies of men, a Houſe of Repreſentatives, and a Senate; ~~each of which ſhall, in all caſes, have a negative on the other. The Legiſlature ſhall meet on the firſt Monday in December in every year.~~

* The legislature shall meet at least once in every year and that meeting shall be on the first Monday in December unless a different day shall be appointed by Law.

IV.

Sect. 1. The Members of the Houſe of Repreſentatives ſhall be choſen every ſecond year, by the people of the ſeveral States comprehended within this Union. The qualifications of the electors ſhall be the ſame, from time to time, as thoſe of the electors in the ſeveral States, of the moſt numerous branch of their own legiſlatures.

Sect. 2. Every Member of the Houſe of Repreſentatives ſhall be of the age of twenty-five years at leaſt; ſhall have been a citizen in the United States for at leaſt ~~three~~ years before his election; and ſhall be, at the time of his election, ~~a reſident~~ of the State in which he ſhall be choſen.

Sect. 3. The Houſe of Repreſentatives ſhall, at its firſt formation, and until the number of citizens and inhabitants ſhall be taken in the manner herein after deſcribed, conſiſt of ſixty-five Members, of whom three ſhall be choſen in New-Hampſhire, eight in Maſſachuſetts, one in Rhode-Iſland and Providence Plantations, five in Connecticut, ſix in New-York, four in New-Jerſey, eight in Pennſylvania, one in Delaware, ſix in Maryland, ten in Virginia, five in North-Carolina, five in South-Carolina, and three in Georgia.

Sect. 4. As the proportions of numbers in the different States will alter from time to time; as ſome of the States may hereafter be divided; as others may be enlarged by addition of territory; as two or more States may be united; as new States will be erected within the limits of the United States, the Legiſlature ſhall, in each of theſe caſes, regulate the number of repreſentatives by the number of inhabitants, according to the ~~[illegible]~~ rate of one for every forty thouſand. Provided that every State shall have at least one representative.

Sect. 5. All bills for raiſing or appropriating money, and for fixing the ſalaries of the officers of government, ſhall originate in the Houſe of Repreſentatives, and ſhall not be altered or amended by the Senate. No money ſhall be drawn from the public Treaſury, but in purſuance of appropriations that ſhall originate in the Houſe of Repreſentatives.

struck out

Sect. 6. The Houſe of Repreſentatives ſhall have the ſole power of impeachment. It ſhall chooſe its Speaker and other officers.

Sect. 7. Vacancies in the Houſe of Repreſentatives ſhall be ſupplied by writs of election from the executive authority of the State, in the repreſentation from which they ſhall happen.

V.

29. *WASHINGTON'S COPY OF THE FIRST PRINTED DRAFT OF THE CONSTITUTION, August 6, 1787, Ratification by the States of the Constitution, RG 360. 15½ x 10½ in. Printed copy of the report of the Committee of Detail, annotated by Washington and others. 7 pages (page 1 illustrated). Endorsed (in Pickering's hand): Printed Draught of the/Constitution, received/from the President of the United/States, March 19. 1796, by/Timothy Pickering/Sec^y of State.*

Ratification of the Constitution

The Constitution presented to the American people in the autumn of 1787 provided the method of its own ratification in its final article. It was to be ratified not by State legislatures but by conventions elected in each State for the express purpose of considering the new Constitution. The nearly moribund Confederation Congress, having roused itself during the summer to pass the Northwest Ordinance, now voted that the Constitution be "transmitted to the several legislatures in order to be submitted to a convention of delegates chosen in each state by the people thereof."

Although the Pennsylvania ratifying convention was the first to meet, the Delaware Convention was the first to ratify the Constitution (document 30). Many of the fears of the small States had been effectively allayed by the equal representation granted the States in the Senate, so that little opposition to the federal plan had developed in Delaware. Elsewhere arguments against the Constitution centered chiefly on three points—that the central government was given too much power, that its power was drawn from the Constitution as the supreme law of the land, and that the Constitution did not contain guarantees of States' rights and individual liberties. The last argument, especially popular, led to general demands for a "bill of rights." There were enough proponents of the new Constitution, however, to ensure its acceptance even though violent discussions raged in several ratifying conventions. In some cases opponents were mollified by a promise that amendments to the Constitution would be proposed as soon as the new government was organized.

When New Hampshire ratified on June 21, 1788, the requirement for ratification by the "conventions of nine States" had been fulfilled so that the Constitution could go into effect. The last of the Original Thirteen to ratify was Rhode Island on May 29, 1790.

The First Presidential Election

The time had now come to put into effect the national electoral process established by the new Constitution, and the Confederation Congress was called upon for a deed of unique self-abnegation: to provide for the election of its own successor. Even though 10 members of Congress had also been members of the Federal Convention, the old Congress debated off and on for 10 weeks, from July 2 to September 28, 1788, what it should do about calling an election. Congress finally passed this resolution:

> . . . That the first Wednesday in January next, be the day for appointing Electors in the several States, which before the said day shall have ratified the said Constitution; that the first Wednesday in February next, be the day for the Electors to assemble in their respective States, and vote for a President; and that the first Wednesday in March next, be the time, and the present Seat of Congress [New York] the place for commencing Proceedings under the said Constitution. (Document 31.)

The Constitution provided only that the Presidential electors should be appointed in whatever manner the legislatures of the individual States directed. In accordance with the congressional resolution fixing January 7, 1789, as the date for choosing electors, Massachusetts acted on that day. The General Court (the legislative body) itself named two electors at large and chose eight from a list of men elected by the voters of the State (document 32). The 10 electors met in the Senate Chamber on February 4, 1789, and, as the Constitution provided, each voted for two men. They cast 10 votes for George Washington and 10 for John Adams.

In South Carolina the legislature named the electors directly. This method was also used by Connecticut, New Jersey, Delaware, and Georgia. Pennsylvania, Maryland, and Virginia chose their electors by popular ballot. New York lost its vote when the two branches of the legislature reached a deadlock over the method to be used. After the seven South Carolina electors had acted, they reported:

> We . . . did vote by ballot for two Persons accordingly, and on opening the said ballots, We found that the Honorable George Washington Esq[r] of Virginia. . . —had seven—votes and John Rutledge—had six—votes and John Hancock had one vote. . . . (Document 33.)

We the Deputies of the People of the Delaware State, in Convention met, having taken into our serious consideration the Fœderal Constitution proposed and agreed upon by the Deputies of the United States in a General Convention held at the City of Philadelphia on the seventeenth day of September in the year of our Lord one thousand seven hundred and eighty seven. Have approved, assented to, ratified, and confirmed, and by these Presents, Do, in virtue of the Power and Authority to us given for that purpose, for and in behalf of ourselves and our Constituents, fully, freely, and entirely approve of, assent to, ratify, and confirm the said Constitution.

Done in Convention at Dover this seventh day of December in the year aforesaid, and in the year of the Independence of the United States of America the twelfth. In Testimony whereof we have hereunto subscribed our Names.

To all whom these Presents shall come Greeting. I Thomas Collins President of the Delaware State do hereby certify that the above instrument of writing is a true copy of the original ratification of the Fœderal Constitution by the Convention of the Delaware State, which original ratification is now in my possession. In Testimony whereof I have caused the seal of the Delaware State to be hereunto annexed.

Thos. Collins

Sussex County	Kent County	New Castle County
John Ingram	Nicholas Ridgely	Jas. Latimer, President
John Jones	Richard Smith	James Black
William Moore	George Truitt	Jno. James
William Hall	Richard Bassett	Gunning Bedford sen.
Thomas Laws	James Sykes	Kensey Johns
Isaac Cooper	Allen McLane	Thomas Watson
Woodman Stockly	Daniel Cummins sen.	Solomon Maxwell
John Laws	Joseph Barker	Nicholas Way
Thomas Evans	Edward White	Thomas Duff
Israel Holland	George Manlove	Gunn. Bedford jun.

30. THE DELAWARE RATIFICATION OF THE CONSTITUTION, *December 7, 1787, Ratification by the States of the Constitution of the United States and of the First Ten Amendments, RG 11. 31⅜ x 16½ in. Parchment. Bears the names of the State deputies, probably in the hand of a clerk. Attested by the signature of Thomas Collins, President of Delaware. State seal in left margin. 1 sheet. Endorsed: Ratification/of the Fœderal Constitution/by the Delaware State/Recorded—page 78./ /Delaware.*

By the United States in Congreſs aſſembled,

SEPTEMBER 13, 1788.

WHEREAS the Convention aſſembled in Philadelphia, purſuant to the Reſolution of Congreſs of the 21ſt February, 1787, did, on the 17th of September in the ſame year, report to the United States in Congreſs aſſembled, a Conſtitution for the People of the United States; whereupon Congreſs, on the 28th of the ſame September, did reſolve unanimouſly, " That the ſaid report, with the Reſolutions and Letter accompanying the ſame, be tranſmitted to the ſeveral Legiſlatures, in order to be ſubmitted to a Convention of Delegates choſen in each State by the people thereof, in conformity to the Reſolves of the Convention made and provided in that caſe:" And whereas the Conſtitution ſo reported by the Convention, and by Congreſs tranſmitted to the ſeveral Legiſlatures, has been ratified in the manner therein declared to be ſufficient for the eſtabliſhment of the ſame, and ſuch Ratifications duly authenticated have been received by Congreſs, and are filed in the Office of the Secretary---therefore,

RESOLVED, That the firſt Wedneſday in January next, be the day for appointing Electors in the ſeveral States, which before the ſaid day ſhall have ratified the ſaid Conſtitution; that the firſt Wedneſday in February next, be the day for the Electors to aſſemble in their reſpective States, and vote for a Preſident; and that the firſt Wedneſday in March next, be the time, and the preſent Seat of Congreſs the place for commencing Proceedings under the ſaid Conſtitution.

31. *CALL FOR THE FIRST PRESIDENTIAL ELECTION, September 13, 1788, Misc. PCC, Broadsides, RG 360. 12⅝ x 7⅞ in. Broadside. 1 page.*

Commonwealth of Massachusetts

In Senate January 7th 1789

Ordered that the Secretary notify

The Honble Caleb Davis

Samuel Phillips junr Esqr

Francis Dana Esqr

Samuel Henshaw Esqr

The Honble William Sever

David Sewall

Walter Spooner

Moses Gill

William Cushing &

William Shepard Esquires, that they have been chosen Electors of President & Vice President of the United States, agreeably to the Constitution thereof & of the time & place of their meeting.

Sent down for concurrence

Saml Phillips junr Presidt

In the House of Representatives January 7th 1789

Read & Concurred

Theodore Sedgwick Spkr

True Copy

Attest — John Avery jun Secretary

32. *APPOINTMENT OF THE MASSACHUSETTS ELECTORS, January 7, 1789, 1A-H1, Election Records, RG 46, Records of the United States Senate. 12 x 7½ in. 1 page. Endorsed: Secretary's Certificate/respecting Electors/ Massachusetts*

City of Charleston State of South Carolina

We the Subscribers being duly appointed in the manner directed by the Legislature of the State of South Carolina Electors for the purpose of chusing a President of the United States of America agreeable to the Federal Constitution did meet at twelve o'Clock on this fourth day of February at the Exchange of the City of Charleston in the State of South Carolina, and being first duly sworn before his Excellency the Governor, agreeably to an Act entitled "an Act prescribing on the part of this State, the times, places and manner of holding Elections for Representatives in the Congress and the manner of appointing Electors of a President of the United States" and having also taken the Oath of Allegiance and Abjuration agreable to the 36th Clause of the Constitution of the State of South Carolina **did** vote by ballot for two Persons accordingly, and on opening the said ballots, we **found** that the Honorable George Washington Esqr. of Virginia — and the Honble John Rutledge Esqr. of South Carolina & the Honble John Hancock Esqr. of Massachusetts — were voted for, and that George Washington — had seven — votes and John Rutledge had six — votes and John Hancock had one vote **all** which we do Certify, and in Testimony thereof have signed our Names and affixed our Seals this fourth day of February in the year of our Lord One thousand seven hundred and Eighty nine, and in the thirteenth year of the Independence of the United States of America

Christ. Gadsden — Edward Rutledge

Henry Laurens — Charles Cotesworth Pinckney

Thos Heyward Junr

Arthur Simkins — John Faucheraud Grimké

33. *REPORT OF THE SOUTH CAROLINA ELECTORAL VOTE, February 4, 1789, 1A-H1, RG 46. 13⅜ x 8⅜ in. Signed by the electors and attested by seals. 1 page.*

The Unanimous Choice

The Confederation Congress had set March 4, 1789, as the date and New York City as the place for the first meeting of Congress under the Constitution, but bad roads and bad weather combined to thwart the best of intentions. Not until April 1 was the House of Representatives organized and not until April 6 did a quorum of the Senate assemble. The first order of business was to count the votes for President and Vice President, and the Senate elected John Langdon as its temporary president solely for that purpose. The electoral votes, counted immediately, showed that each of the 69 electors had voted for George Washington. He was thus the unanimous choice for the Presidency. John Adams, who received the next largest number of votes, was elected to the Vice Presidency. That same day Langdon wrote to Washington and Adams informing them of this result. The letter to Washington read:

> I have the honor to transmit to your Excellency the information of your unanimous election to the office of President of the United States of America. Suffer me, Sir, to indulge the hope, that so auspicious a mark of public confidence will meet your approbation, and be considered as a sure pledge of the affection and support you are to expect from a free and an enlightened People—(Document 34.)

Charles Thomson, the faithful Secretary of every Congress beginning with the First Continental Congress of 1774, was chosen to carry the letter of notification to Mount Vernon. Typical of the man whose meticulous records were invaluable to the incoming Presidential administration and to historians ever since, Thomson's description of his journey and Washington's remarks upon learning of his election is detailed and factual:

> In pursuance of the orders I received from the Senate I left New york on tuesday the seventh of the present month; and though much impeded by tempestuous weather, bad roads and the many large rivers I had to cross, yet by unremitted diligence I reached Mount Vernon, the seat of his excellency genl Washington on tuesday the 14 about 12 o clock. I found his excellency at home and after communicating to him the object of my mission and the substance of my instructions I took an opportunity, on the day of my arrival, to address him. . . .
>
> . . . his Excellency was pleased to make the following reply "Sir, I have been long accustomed to entertain so great a respect for the opinion of my fellow citizens, that the knowledge of their unanimous suffrages having been given in my favour scarcely leaves me the alternative for an Option. Whatever may have been my private feelings and sentiments, I believe I cannot give a greater evidence of my sensibility for the honor they have done me than by accepting the appointment
>
> I am so much affected by this fresh proof of my country's esteem and confidence, that silence can best explain my gratitude—While I realize the arduous nature of the task which is conferred on me and feel my inability to perform it, I wish there may not be reason for regreting the choice. All I can promise is only that which can be accomplished by an honest zeal. . . ." (Document 35.)

Washington left Mount Vernon for New York on April 16. His journey was almost a triumphal procession, as the American people sought to do him honor along the way. On April 30 on the balcony of Federal Hall in Wall Street, the oath of office prescribed in the new Constitution was administered to Washington by Robert R. Livingston, the chancellor of New York State, before a large and enthusiastic crowd of citizens in the street below. Then the new President entered the Senate Chamber, where he delivered an inaugural address to Congress. He said in part:

> Among the vicissitudes incident to life, no event could have filled me with greater anxieties than that of which the notification was transmitted by your order. . . . On the one hand, I was summoned by my Country, whose voice I can never hear but with veneration and love. . . . On the other hand, the magnitude and difficulty of the trust to which the voice of my Country called me, being sufficient to awaken in the wisest and most experienced of her citizens, a distrustful scrutiny into his qualifications, could not but overwhelm with dispondence, one, who, inheriting inferior endowments from nature and unpractised in the duties of civil administration, ought to be peculiarly conscious of his own deficiencies. . . .
>
> Such being the impressions under which I have . . . repaired to the present station; it would be peculiarly improper to omit in this first official Act, my fervent supplications to that Almighty Being who rules over the Universe . . . that his benediction may consecrate to the liberties and happiness of the People of the United States, a Government instituted by themselves for these essential purposes. . . . (Document 36.)

Copy

New York, 6th April, 1789.

Sir,

I have the honor to transmit to your Excellency the information of your unanimous election to the office of President of the United States of America. Suffer me, Sir, to indulge the hope, that so auspicious a mark of public confidence will meet your approbation, and be considered as a sure pledge of the affection and support you are to expect from a free and an enlightened People.

I am, Sir, with
sentiments of respect,
Yr. Ob. Servt.
J L

His Excellency
George Washington, Esqr.

34. *LETTER INFORMING WASHINGTON OF HIS ELECTION AS PRESIDENT*, April 6, 1789, 1A-J3, *Papers Pertaining to the Notification of the President and Vice President of Their Election, RG 46. 12¾ x 7⅞ in. Official Copy. On the back of this page is the Official Copy of the Notification to John Adams of his election as Vice President. 1 page. Endorsed: Ist Sess: L Ist Con:/Copies to/The President & /Vice President/Entd/New York/April 6th/ 1789./ /L. Jour:/fol 10 & 11.*

New-york April 24. 1789

Sir,

In pursuance of the orders I received from the Senate I left New york on tuesday the seventh of the present month, and though much impeded by tempestuous weather, bad roads, and the many large rivers I had to cross, yet by unremitted diligence I reached Mount Vernon, the seat of his excellency genl Washington on tuesday the 14 about 12 o clock. I found his excellency at home and after communicating to him the object of my mission and the substance of my instructions I took an opportunity, on the day of my arrival, to address him as follows

" Sir, The president of the Senate, chosen for the special occasion, having opened and counted the votes of the Electors in the presence of the Senate and the house of Representatives, I was honored with the commands of the Senate to wait upon your Excellency with the information of your being elected to the office of President of the United States of America. This commission was entrusted to me on account of my having been long in the confidence of the late Congress and charged with the duties of one of the principal civil departments of Government.

I have now, Sir, to inform you, that the proofs you have given of your patriotism and of your readiness to sacrifice domestic ease and private enjoyments to preserve the liberty and promote the happiness of your country did not permit the two houses to harbour a doubt of your undertaking this great, this important office, to which you are called not only by the unanimous votes of the electors but by the voice of America, I have it therefore in command to accompany you to New york where the Senate and the house of representatives are convened

35. *THOMSON's LETTER ON HIS JOURNEY TO MOUNT VERNON,* April 24, 1789, 1A-J3, RG 46. 12¾ x 8 in. In the hand of Charles Thomson. 3 pages (pages 1 and 2 illustrated). Endorsed: Apr 24/Legis: I. Cong: I. Sess:/Report of Charles/Thompson Esq. on the/mode of his address-/ing and notifying Gen./Washington, of his e-/lection, as president/of the U.S. of A./April 24./1789./No 10//1st Sess: 1st Con L/April 24th 1789/Charles Thomson/Read & ordered to lie/on file. End/Fol:31.

for the dispatch of public business. In executing this part of my commission, where personal gratification coincides with duty I shall wait your time and be wholly governed by your convenience".

To this his Excellency was pleased to make the following reply "Sir, I have been long accustomed to entertain so great a respect for the opinion of my fellow citizens, that the knowledge of their unanimous suffrages having been given in my favour scarcely leaves me the alternative for an Option. Whatever may have been my private feelings and sentiments, I believe I cannot give a greater evidence of my sensibility for the honor they have done me than by accepting the appointment

I am so much affected by this fresh proof of my country's esteem and confidence, that silence can best explain my gratitude — While I realize the arduous nature of the task which is conferred on me and feel my inability to perform it, I wish there may not be reason for regreting the choice. All I can promise is only that which can be accomplished by an honest zeal.

Upon considering how long time some of the gentlemen of both houses of Congress have been at New york, how anxiously desirous they must be to proceed to business and how deeply the public mind appears to be impressed with the necessity of doing it immediately I cannot find myself at liberty to delay my Journey — I shall therefore be in readiness to set out the day after to morrow, and shall be happy in the pleasure of your company. For you will permit me to say that it was a peculiar gratification to have received the communication from you"

His Excellency set out accordingly on thursday the 16th His progress was retarded by the tender and affectionate leave which his neighbours and friends took of him; by the congratulatory addresses which he was obliged to receive by the way; and by the testimonies of public esteem and joy, to which it was necessary for him to pay attention, in the several states through which he

(Continuation of Document 35)

Fellow Citizens of the Senate
and
of the House of Representatives.

Among the vicissitudes
incident to life, no event could have
filled me with greater anxieties than
that of which the notification was
transmitted by your order, and received on the fourteenth day of the
present month: — On the one hand,
I was summoned by my Country, whose
voice I can never hear but with venera-
tion and love, from a retreat which
I had chosen with the fondest prede-
lection, and, in my flattering hopes,
with an immutable decision, as the
asylum of my declining years: a retreat which was rendered every day
more necessary as well as more dear
to me, by the addition of habit to in-
clination, and of frequent interrup-
tions in my health to the gradual waste
committed on it by time. — On the
other hand, the magnitude and dif-
ficulty of the trust to which the voice
of my Country called me, being sufficient to awaken in the wisest and most
experienced of her citizens, a distrust
ful

36. *WASHINGTON'S INAUGURAL ADDRESS, April 30, 1789, 1A-E1, President's Messages, RG 46. In the hand of George Washington. 8 pages (pages 1 and 8 illustrated). Endorsed: The Presidents/Speech/30 April./1789/ Ent:/fol:35 N° 7*

permanent provision for the Executive Department; and must accordingly pray that the pecuniary estimates for the Station in which I am placed, may, during my continuance in it, be limited to such actual expenditures as the public good may be thought to require.—

Having thus imparted to you my sentiments, as they have been awakened by the occasion which brings us together, I shall take my present leave; but not without resorting once more to the benign Parent of the human race, in humble supplication that since he has been pleased to favour the American people, with opportunities for deliberating in perfect tranquility, and dispositions for deciding with unparellelled unanimity on a form of Government, for the security of their Union, and the advancement of their happiness; so his divine blessing may be equally conspicuous in the enlarged views, the temperate consultations, and the wise measures on which the success of this Government must depend.—

G. Washington

The President's Speech · 30 April. 1789.

(Continuation of Document 36)

The Bill of Rights

One step remained, one promise still had to be kept, before the formation of the Union was complete. One of the most frequent objections to the Constitution during the debate over its ratification was that it lacked specific guarantees of the personal freedom of individual citizens and the rights of the States. The State ratifying conventions in Massachusetts, South Carolina, New Hampshire, Virginia, and New York submitted proposed amendments with their resolutions of ratification. Proponents of the document promised that a "bill of rights" would be proposed by the new Government as soon as it was organized.

In North Carolina the struggle over ratification was even more severe, for no mere promise was satisfactory to its convention. Meeting in Hillsboro on August 1, 1788, the convention passed a resolution:

> . . . That a Declaration of Rights, asserting and securing from incroachment the great Principles of civil and religious Liberty, and the unalienable Rights of the People, together with Amendments to the most ambiguous and exceptionable Parts of the said Constitution of Government, ought to be laid before Congress, and the Convention of the States that shall or may be called for the Purpose of Amending the said Constitution, for their consideration, previous to the Ratification of the Constitution aforesaid, on the part of the State of North Carolina. (Document 37.)

The resolution was followed by 26 suggested amendments. The convention then adjourned without taking final action on the Constitution.

Soon after the First Congress met, it began to consider amendments guaranteeing civil rights and liberties. James Madison, then a Representative from Virginia, had pledged to use his influence to bring about the adoption of a "bill of rights." From the many amendments that had been suggested by ratifying conventions he offered on June 8, 1789, a select list for the consideration of the House. The House passed 17 of these. The Senate reduced this number to 12 by combining some and deleting others.

On September 25, 1789, Congress passed a resolution proposing 12 constitutional amendments. The enrolled original of the resolution—the Federal Government's official copy—was signed by Augustus Muhlenberg, Speaker of the House, and John Adams, President of the Senate. Thirteen other signed copies, also written on parchment, were forwarded to President Washington; and on October 2, in pursuance of a congressional resolution, he transmitted a copy to each State of the Union and to Rhode Island and North Carolina which still had not ratified the Constitution and could take no formal action on the amendments at that time. However, the main objection of North Carolina to the Constitution was removed. Another convention was held; and on November 22, 1789, North Carolina ratified the Constitution and thus became a member of the Union.

The suggested amendments were well received by the other States as well, and some of them immediately acted on ratification. New York ratified on March 27, 1790 (document 38), accepting all the suggested amendments except the second. While the proposed amendments were under consideration by the States, Rhode Island and the new State of Vermont joined the Union. This raised to 11 the number of States necessary to make a change in the Constitution. On December 15, 1791, Virginia ratified all the proposed amendments. Of the original 12 proposed, 10 amendments had then been ratified by the requisite three-fourths of the States. These amendments, guaranteeing civil rights and liberties to the individual, thus became part of the fundamental law of the land.

State of North-Carolina.

IN CONVENTION, AUGUST 1, 1788.

Reſolved, That a Declaration of Rights, aſſerting and ſecuring from incroachment the great Principles of civil and religious Liberty, and the unalienable Rights of the People, together with Amendments to the moſt ambiguous and exceptionable Parts of the ſaid Conſtitution of Government, ought to be laid before Congreſs, and the Convention of the States that ſhall or may be called for the Purpoſe of Amending the ſaid Conſtitution, for their conſideration, previous to the Ratification of the Conſtitution aforeſaid, on the part of the State of North Carolina.

DECLARATION OF RIGHTS.

1ſt That there are certain natural rights of which men, when they form a ſocial compact, cannot deprive or diveſt their poſterity, among which are the enjoyment of life, and liberty, with the means of acquiring, poſſeſſing and protecting property, and purſuing and obtaining happineſs and ſafety.

2d. That all power is naturally veſted in, and conſequently derived from the people; that magiſtrates therefore are their truſtees, and agents, and at all times amenable to them.

3d. That Government ought to be inſtituted for the common benefit, protection and ſecurity of the people; and that the doctrine of non-reſiſtance againſt arbitrary power and oppreſſion is abſurd, ſlaviſh, and deſtructive to the good and happineſs of mankind.

4th That no man or ſet of men are entitled to excluſive or ſeparate public emoluments or privileges from the community, but in conſideration of public ſervices; which not being deſcendible, neither ought the offices of magiſtrate, legiſlator or judge, or any other public office to be hereditary.

5th. That the legiſlative, executive and judiciary powers of government ſhould be ſeparate and diſtinct, and that the members of the two firſt may be reſtrained from oppreſſion by feeling and participating the public burthens, they ſhould at fixed periods be reduced to a private ſtation, return into the maſs of the people; and the vacancies be ſupplied by certain and regular elections; in which all or any part of the former members to be eligible or ineligible, as the rules of the Conſtitution of Government, and the laws ſhall direct.

6th. That elections of Repreſentatives in the legiſlature ought to be free and frequent, and all men having ſufficient evidence of permanent common intereſt with, and attachment to the community, ought to have the right of ſuffrage: and no aid, charge, tax or fee can be ſet, rated, or levied upon the people without their own conſent, or that of their repreſentatives, ſo elected, nor can they be bound by any law, to which they have not in like manner aſſented for the public good.

7th. That all power of ſuſpending laws, or the execution of laws by any authority without the conſent of the repreſentatives, of the people in the Legiſlature, is injurious to their rights, and ought not to be exerciſed.

8th. That in all capital and criminal proſecutions, a man hath a right to demand the cauſe and nature of his accuſation, to be confronted with the accuſers and witneſſes, to call for evidence and be allowed counſel in his favor, and to a fair and ſpeedy trial by an impartial jury of his vicinage, without whoſe unanimous conſent he cannot be found guilty (except in the government of the land and naval forces) nor can he be compelled to give evidence againſt himſelf.

9th. That no freeman ought to be taken, impriſoned, or diſſeized of his freehold, liberties, privileges or franchiſes, or outlawed or exiled, or in any manner deſtroyed or deprived of his life, liberty, or property but by the law of the land.

10th. That every freeman reſtrained of his liberty is entitled to a remedy to enquire into the lawfulneſs thereof, and to remove the ſame, if unlawful, and that ſuch remedy ought not to be denied nor delayed.

11th. That in controverſies reſpecting property, and in ſuits between man and man, the ancient trial by jury is one of the greateſt ſecurities to the rights of the people, and ought to remain ſacred and inviolable.

12th. That every freeman ought to find a certain remedy by recourſe to the laws for all injuries and wrongs he may receive in his perſon, property, or character. He ought to obtain right and juſtice freely without ſale, completely and without denial, promptly and without delay, and that all eſtabliſhments, or regulations contravening theſe rights, are oppreſſive and unjuſt.

13th. That exceſſive bail ought not to be required, nor exceſſive fines impoſed, nor cruel and unuſual puniſhments inflicted,

14. That every freeman has a right to be ſecure from all unreaſonable ſearches, and ſeizures of his perſon, his papers, and property: all warrants therefore to ſearch ſuſpected places, or ſeize any freeman, his papers or property, without information upon oath (or affirmation of a perſon religiouſly ſcrupulous of taking an oath) of legal and ſufficient cauſe, are grievous and oppreſſive, and all general warrants to ſearch ſuſpected places, or to apprehend any ſuſpected perſon without ſpecially naming or deſcribing the place or perſon, are dangerous and ought not to be granted.

15th. That the people have a right peaceably to aſſemble together to conſult for the common good, or to inſtruct their repreſentatives; and that every freeman has a right to petition or apply to the Legiſlature for redreſs of grievances.

16th. That the people have a right to freedom of ſpeech, and of writing and publiſhing their ſentiments; that the freedom of the preſs is one of the greateſt bulwarks of Liberty, and ought not to be violated.

17th. That the people have a right to keep and bear arms; that a well regulated militia compoſed of the body of the people, trained to arms, is the proper, natural and ſafe defence of a free ſtate. That ſtanding armies in time of peace aro dangerous to Liberty, and therefore ought to be avoided, as far as the circumſtances and protection of the community will admit; and that in all caſes, the military ſhould be under ſtrict ſubordination to, and governed by the civil power.

18th. That no ſoldier in time of peace ought to be quartered in any houſe without the conſent of the owner, and in time of war in ſuch manner only as the Laws direct.

19th. That any perſon religiouſly ſcrupulous of bearing arms ought to be exempted upon payment of an equivalent to employ another to bears arms in his ſtead.

10. That religion, or the duty which we owe to our Creator, and the manner of diſcharging it, can be directed only by reaſon and conviction, not by force or violence, and therefore all men have an equal, natural and unalienable right to the free exerciſe of religion according to the dictates of conſcience, and that no particular religious ſect or ſociety ought to be favoured or eſtabliſhed by law in preference to others.

Amendments to the Conſtitution.

I. THAT each ſtate in the union ſhall, reſpectively, retain every power, juriſdiction and right, which is not by this conſtitution delegated to the Congreſs of the United States, or to the departments of the Federal Government.

37. *NORTH CAROLINA'S PROPOSED AMENDMENTS TO THE CONSTITUTION, August 1, 1788, Ratification by the States of the Constitution, RG 11. 12-5/16 x 7⅜ in. Bears signatures of Samuel Johnson, President, and J. Hunt, Secretary, of the North Carolina Convention. 2 pages. Endorsed: Proceedings of the/Convention of the State of/North Carolina/Receiv'd September 13th 1788/Enter'd page 167 & 179*

The People of the State of New York, by the Grace of God, Free and Independent To all to whom these presents shall come or may concern, Greeting: Know Ye, that We having inspected the Records remaining in our Secretary's Office do find there a certain Act of our Legislature in the words and figures following "An Act ratifying certain Articles in addition to and amendment "of the Constitution of the United States of America proposed by the Congress. Whereas by the fifth article of the Constitution of the United States of America, it is provided that the Congress whenever two thirds of both "Houses shall deem it necessary shall propose amendments to the said Constitution which shall be valid to all intents and purposes as part of the said Constitution when ratified by the Legislatures of three fourths of the "several States, or by Conventions in three fourths thereof as the one or the other mode of ratification may be proposed by the Congress. And whereas in the Session of the Congress of the United States of America "begun and held at the City of New York on Wednesday the fourth of March one thousand seven hundred and eighty nine it was resolved by the Senate and House of Representatives of the United States of America "in Congress assembled two thirds of both Houses concurring, That the following articles be proposed to the Legislatures of the several States as amendments to the Constitution of the United States, all or any of which "articles when ratified by three fourths of the said Legislatures to be valid to all intents and purposes as part of the said Constitution Vizt Articles in addition to and amendment of the Constitution of the United States "of America proposed by Congress and ratified by the Legislatures of the several States pursuant to the fifth article of the original Constitution. Article the First.. After the first Enumeration required by the first article of the "Constitution there shall be one Representative for every thirty thousand until the number shall amount to one hundred, after which the proportion shall be so regulated by Congress that there shall be not less than one hundred "Representatives, nor less than one Representative for every forty thousand persons until the number of Representatives shall amount to two hundred, after which the proportion shall be so regulated by Congress that there "shall not be less than two hundred Representatives, nor more than one Representative for every fifty thousand persons. Article the Second.. No Law, varying the Compensation for the Services of the Senators "and Representatives, shall take effect until an Election of Representatives shall have intervened. Article the Third.. Congress shall make no law respecting an Establishment of Religion or prohibiting the free ex- "ercise thereof, or abridging the freedom of Speech or of the press, or the right of the People peaceably to assemble and to petition the Government for a redress of grievances. Article the Fourth.. A well regulated militia being "necessary to the Security of a free State, the right of the People to keep and bear arms shall not be infringed. Article the Fifth.. No Soldier shall, in time of Peace, be quartered in any house without the consent of the Owner, nor in "time of war, but in a manner to be prescribed by law. Article the Sixth.. The right of the People to be secure in their persons, houses, papers, and effects against unreasonable searches and seizures shall not be violated, and "no warrants shall issue but upon probable cause supported by oath or affirmation, and particularly describing the place to be searched and the persons or things to be seized. Article the Seventh.. No person shall be "held to answer for a capital or otherwise infamous crime, unless on a presentment or Indictment of a grand Jury, except in cases arising in the land or naval forces, or in the militia when in actual Service in time of War or public danger "nor shall any person be subject for the same offence to be twice put in jeopardy of life or limb nor shall be compelled in any criminal case to be a Witness against himself, nor be deprived of life, liberty, or property without due process of law "nor shall private property be taken for public use without just compensation. Article the Eighth.. In all criminal prosecutions the accused shall enjoy the right to a speedy and public trial by an impartial Jury of the State and "district wherein the Crime shall have been committed, which district shall have been previously ascertained by law, and to be informed of the nature and cause of the accusation, to be confronted with the Witnesses against him, to have compulsory process "for obtaining Witnesses in his favor, and to have the assistance of Counsel for his defence. Article the Ninth.. In Suits at Common Law where the value in controversy shall exceed twenty dollars, the right of trial by Jury shall be preserved and "no fact tried by a Jury shall be otherwise re-examined in any Court of the United States, than according to the rules of the Common Law. Article the Tenth.. Excessive bail shall not be required nor excessive fines imposed, nor cruel and "unusual punishments inflicted. Article the Eleventh.. The Enumeration in the Constitution of certain rights shall not be construed to deny or disparage others retained by the people. Article the Twelfth.. The pow- "ers not delegated to the United States by the Constitution, nor prohibited by it to the States, are reserved to the States respectively, or to the people. And whereas the Legislature of this State have considered the said Articles and do agree "to the same, except the Second Article: Therefore Be it Enacted by the People of the State of New York represented in Senate and Assembly and it is hereby enacted by the authority of the same that the said Articles, except the second, "shall be and hereby are ratified by the Legislature of this State. State of New York In Assembly February 22d 1790. This Bill having been read the third time, Resolved that the Bill do pass By order of the Assembly, Gulian Verplanck "Speaker. State of New York, In Senate Febru.y 24th 1790 This Bill having been read a third time, Resolved that the Bill do pass, By order of the Senate Isaac Roosevelt President, pro hac vice. Council of Revision, 27th Fe- "bruary 1790, Resolved that it does not appear improper to the Council that this Bill entitled "An Act ratifying certain articles in addition to and amendment of the Constitution of the United States of America proposed by the Congress" should "become a Law of this State Geo: Clinton." All which We have caused to be Exemplified by these presents: In Testimony whereof We have caused these our Letters to be made patent and the great Seal of our said State to be hereunto affixed: Witness our Trusty and wellbeloved George Clinton Esquire, Governor of our said State, General and Commander in Chief of all the Militia and admiral of the Navy of the same, at our City of New York the twenty seventh day of March in the Year one thousand seven hundred and Ninety, and in the fourteenth Year of our Independence.

Geo: Clinton

38. *NEW YORK'S RATIFICATION OF THE BILL OF RIGHTS*, March 27, 1790, ibid., RG 11. 29⅜ x 14⅞ in. Diameter of Seal 3⅜ in. Parchment. Signed by George Clinton, Governor of New York, with the State seal appended. 1 sheet. Endorsed: Passed the Secretary's Office/the 27th March 1790—/Lewis A. Scott, Secretary.

A Note on the Documents

When the First Continental Congress met on September 5, 1774, in Philadelphia, one of its earliest acts was to elect Charles Thomson Secretary of the Congress. He served in this capacity for both the Continental Congress and its successor, the Congress of the Confederation for 15 years—until the establishment of the Federal Government in 1789. Thanks to Thomson's conscientious care, the "Papers of the Continental Congress," now in the National Archives, provide modern historians with a rich record of the events of the formative years of the United States.

Very important among the "PCC" are the Journals of the Continental and Confederation Congresses, of which there are three versions. The "Rough Journal" is Thomson's daily record of the order of business; the "Corrected" or "Transcript" Journal is the Rough Journal edited for publication by committees appointed from time to time for this purpose; and the several "Secret Journals" record secret proceedings of the Congress.

The variety of other papers in this body of records attests to the breadth of the concerns of the Congress. For example, there are original and transcript letters and reports from such figures as George Washington, John Hancock, Benjamin Franklin, and many other military and civil officials of the United States. In addition there are dispatches from American representatives abroad and notes from foreign envoys in the United States, as well as memorials and petitions to Congress showing the concerns of the American people during the period. In the letters received from Governors and other officials of the States, the activities of the States and their relation to Congress are revealed. Foreign affairs, government finance, military and naval problems, relations with Indians, land distribution and many other areas of pre-Federal history are represented in the Papers of the Continental Congress.

In 1789, the PCC were turned over to the Department of Foreign Affairs (later the Department of State) of the Washington administration. During the War of 1812, they narrowly escaped destruction by being transported out of the city when the British burned Washington.

From 1815 to 1903, the Papers of the Continental Congress remained in the custody of the State Department. Their transfer to the Library of Congress in 1903 was partially an attempt to make them more accessible to scholars. Since President Theodore Roosevelt's Executive Order covering the transfer allowed the State Department to select which papers should be placed in the Library, it was decided to keep at the State Department the papers relating to diplomatic history and the "great documents," including the Declaration of Independence, the Articles of Confederation, the Ordinance of 1787, the Constitution, and the Bill of Rights. However, President Warren G. Harding ordered that the "Great Charters" be added to the PCC held by the Library of Congress, and in 1924 the Declaration of Independence and the Constitution were placed on public display on the second floor of the Library.

When in 1938 the State Department transferred sections of its records to the newly created National Archives, the first of the Papers of the Continental Congress found their way into the National Archives. The Library of Congress released the bulk of the Papers of the Continental Congress to the National Archives 14 years later, thereby reuniting this famous body of records in the depository designed to keep the permanently valuable records of the Federal Government.

With the records of the Constitutional Convention, they constitute Record Group 360, The Records of the Continental and Confederation Congresses and the Constitutional Convention, in the Legislative, Judicial and Diplomatic Records Division of the National Archives. Most of the documents reproduced in this publication and in the accompanying facsimile package are from this Record Group. All are among the records in the National Archives Building in Washington.

In the citations in this essay, the following abbreviations have been used:

PCC—Papers of the Continental Congress

RG—Record Group

Lengthy quotations in the text for which no citation is given are from the record of the appropriate day's proceedings as printed in the 34-volume edition of the *Journals of the Continental Congress* produced by the Library of Congress (Washington, D.C.: Government Printing Office, 1904-37).

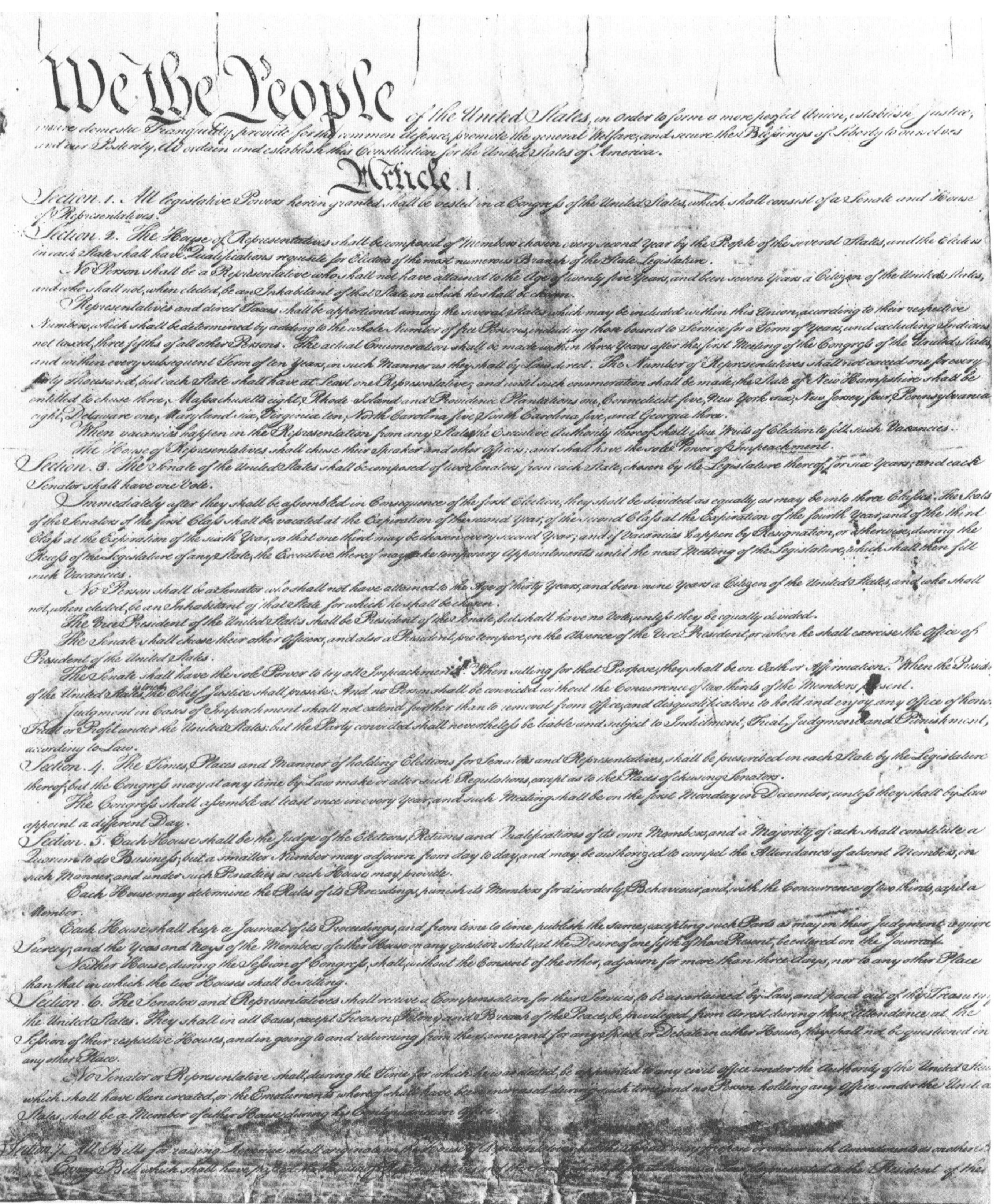

We the People of the United States, in Order to form a more perfect Union, establish Justice, insure domestic Tranquility, provide for the common defence, promote the general Welfare, and secure the Blessings of Liberty to ourselves and our Posterity, do ordain and establish this Constitution for the United States of America.

Article. I.

Section. 1. All legislative Powers herein granted shall be vested in a Congress of the United States, which shall consist of a Senate and House of Representatives.

Section. 2. The House of Representatives shall be composed of Members chosen every second Year by the People of the several States, and the Electors in each State shall have the Qualifications requisite for Electors of the most numerous Branch of the State Legislature.

No Person shall be a Representative who shall not have attained to the Age of twenty five Years, and been seven Years a Citizen of the United States, and who shall not, when elected, be an Inhabitant of that State in which he shall be chosen.

Representatives and direct Taxes shall be apportioned among the several States which may be included within this Union, according to their respective Numbers, which shall be determined by adding to the whole Number of free Persons, including those bound to Service for a Term of Years, and excluding Indians not taxed, three fifths of all other Persons. The actual Enumeration shall be made within three Years after the first Meeting of the Congress of the United States, and within every subsequent Term of ten Years, in such Manner as they shall by Law direct. The Number of Representatives shall not exceed one for every thirty Thousand, but each State shall have at Least one Representative; and until such enumeration shall be made, the State of New Hampshire shall be entitled to chuse three, Massachusetts eight, Rhode-Island and Providence Plantations one, Connecticut five, New-York six, New Jersey four, Pennsylvania eight, Delaware one, Maryland six, Virginia ten, North Carolina five, South Carolina five, and Georgia three.

When vacancies happen in the Representation from any State, the Executive Authority thereof shall issue Writs of Election to fill such Vacancies.

The House of Representatives shall chuse their Speaker and other Officers; and shall have the sole Power of Impeachment.

Section. 3. The Senate of the United States shall be composed of two Senators from each State, chosen by the Legislature thereof, for six Years; and each Senator shall have one Vote.

Immediately after they shall be assembled in Consequence of the first Election, they shall be divided as equally as may be into three Classes. The Seats of the Senators of the first Class shall be vacated at the Expiration of the second Year, of the second Class at the Expiration of the fourth Year, and of the third Class at the Expiration of the sixth Year, so that one third may be chosen every second Year; and if Vacancies happen by Resignation, or otherwise, during the Recess of the Legislature of any State, the Executive thereof may make temporary Appointments until the next Meeting of the Legislature, which shall then fill such Vacancies.

No Person shall be a Senator who shall not have attained to the Age of thirty Years, and been nine Years a Citizen of the United States, and who shall not, when elected, be an Inhabitant of that State for which he shall be chosen.

The Vice President of the United States shall be President of the Senate, but shall have no Vote, unless they be equally divided.

The Senate shall chuse their other Officers, and also a President pro tempore, in the Absence of the Vice President, or when he shall exercise the Office of President of the United States.

The Senate shall have the sole Power to try all Impeachments. When sitting for that Purpose, they shall be on Oath or Affirmation. When the President of the United States is tried, the Chief Justice shall preside: And no Person shall be convicted without the Concurrence of two thirds of the Members present.

Judgment in Cases of Impeachment shall not extend further than to removal from Office, and disqualification to hold and enjoy any Office of honor, Trust or Profit under the United States: but the Party convicted shall nevertheless be liable and subject to Indictment, Trial, Judgment and Punishment, according to Law.

Section. 4. The Times, Places and Manner of holding Elections for Senators and Representatives, shall be prescribed in each State by the Legislature thereof; but the Congress may at any time by Law make or alter such Regulations, except as to the Places of chusing Senators.

The Congress shall assemble at least once in every Year, and such Meeting shall be on the first Monday in December, unless they shall by Law appoint a different Day.

Section. 5. Each House shall be the Judge of the Elections, Returns and Qualifications of its own Members, and a Majority of each shall constitute a Quorum to do Business; but a smaller Number may adjourn from day to day, and may be authorized to compel the Attendance of absent Members, in such Manner, and under such Penalties as each House may provide.

Each House may determine the Rules of its Proceedings, punish its Members for disorderly Behaviour, and, with the Concurrence of two thirds, expel a Member.

Each House shall keep a Journal of its Proceedings, and from time to time publish the same, excepting such Parts as may in their Judgment require Secrecy; and the Yeas and Nays of the Members of either House on any question shall, at the Desire of one fifth of those Present, be entered on the Journal.

Neither House, during the Session of Congress, shall, without the Consent of the other, adjourn for more than three days, nor to any other Place than that in which the two Houses shall be sitting.

Section. 6. The Senators and Representatives shall receive a Compensation for their Services, to be ascertained by Law, and paid out of the Treasury of the United States. They shall in all Cases, except Treason, Felony and Breach of the Peace, be privileged from Arrest during their Attendance at the Session of their respective Houses, and in going to and returning from the same; and for any Speech or Debate in either House, they shall not be questioned in any other Place.

No Senator or Representative shall, during the Time for which he was elected, be appointed to any civil Office under the Authority of the United States, which shall have been created, or the Emoluments whereof shall have been encreased during such time; and no Person holding any Office under the United States, shall be a Member of either House during his Continuance in Office.

Section. 7. All Bills for raising Revenue shall originate in the House of Representatives; but the Senate may propose or concur with Amendments as on other Bills.

Every Bill which shall have passed the [illegible] be presented to the President of the

THE CONSTITUTION OF THE UNITED STATES

United States; If he approve he shall sign it, but if not he shall return it, with his Objections to that House in which it shall have originated, who shall enter the Objections at large on their Journal, and proceed to reconsider it. If after such Reconsideration two thirds of that House shall agree to pass the Bill, it shall be sent, together with the Objections, to the other House, by which it shall likewise be reconsidered, and if approved by two thirds of that House, it shall become a Law. But in all such Cases the Votes of both Houses shall be determined by yeas and Nays, and the Names of the Persons voting for and against the Bill shall be entered on the Journal of each House respectively. If any Bill shall not be returned by the President within ten Days (Sundays excepted) after it shall have been presented to him, the Same shall be a Law, in like Manner as if he had signed it, unless the Congress by their Adjournment prevent its Return, in which Case it shall not be a Law.

Every Order, Resolution, or Vote to which the Concurrence of the Senate and House of Representatives may be necessary (except on a question of Adjournment) shall be presented to the President of the United States; and before the Same shall take Effect, shall be approved by him, or being disapproved by him, shall be repassed by two thirds of the Senate and House of Representatives, according to the Rules and Limitations prescribed in the Case of a Bill.

Section. 8. The Congress shall have Power To lay and collect Taxes, Duties, Imposts and Excises, to pay the Debts and provide for the common Defence and general Welfare of the United States; but all Duties, Imposts and Excises shall be uniform throughout the United States;

To borrow Money on the credit of the United States;

To regulate Commerce with foreign Nations, and among the several States, and with the Indian Tribes;

To establish an uniform Rule of Naturalization, and uniform Laws on the subject of Bankruptcies throughout the United States;

To coin Money, regulate the Value thereof, and of foreign Coin, and fix the Standard of Weights and Measures;

To provide for the Punishment of counterfeiting the Securities and current Coin of the United States;

To establish Post Offices and post Roads;

To promote the Progress of Science and useful Arts, by securing for limited Times to Authors and Inventors the exclusive Right to their respective Writings and Discoveries;

To constitute Tribunals inferior to the supreme Court;

To define and punish Piracies and Felonies committed on the high Seas, and Offences against the Law of Nations;

To declare War, grant Letters of Marque and Reprisal, and make Rules concerning Captures on Land and Water;

To raise and support Armies, but no Appropriation of Money to that Use shall be for a longer Term than two Years;

To provide and maintain a Navy;

To make Rules for the Government and Regulation of the land and naval Forces;

To provide for calling forth the Militia to execute the Laws of the Union, suppress Insurrections and repel Invasions;

To provide for organizing, arming, and disciplining, the Militia, and for governing such Part of them as may be employed in the Service of the United States, reserving to the States respectively, the Appointment of the Officers, and the Authority of training the Militia according to the discipline prescribed by Congress;

To exercise exclusive Legislation in all Cases whatsoever, over such District (not exceeding ten Miles square) as may, by Cession of particular States, and the Acceptance of Congress, become the Seat of the Government of the United States, and to exercise like Authority over all Places purchased by the Consent of the Legislature of the State in which the Same shall be, for the Erection of Forts, Magazines, Arsenals, dock-Yards, and other needful Buildings;—And

To make all Laws which shall be necessary and proper for carrying into Execution the foregoing Powers, and all other Powers vested by this Constitution in the Government of the United States, or in any Department or Officer thereof.

Section. 9. The Migration or Importation of such Persons as any of the States now existing shall think proper to admit, shall not be prohibited by the Congress prior to the Year one thousand eight hundred and eight, but a Tax or duty may be imposed on such Importation, not exceeding ten dollars for each Person.

The Privilege of the Writ of Habeas Corpus shall not be suspended, unless when in Cases of Rebellion or Invasion the public Safety may require it.

No Bill of Attainder or ex post facto Law shall be passed.

No Capitation, or other direct, Tax shall be laid, unless in Proportion to the Census or Enumeration herein before directed to be taken.

No Tax or Duty shall be laid on Articles exported from any State.

No Preference shall be given by any Regulation of Commerce or Revenue to the Ports of one State over those of another: nor shall Vessels bound to, or from, one State, be obliged to enter, clear, or pay Duties in another.

No Money shall be drawn from the Treasury, but in Consequence of Appropriations made by Law; and a regular Statement and Account of the Receipts and Expenditures of all public Money shall be published from time to time.

No Title of Nobility shall be granted by the United States: And no Person holding any Office of Profit or Trust under them, shall, without the Consent of the Congress, accept of any present, Emolument, Office, or Title, of any kind whatever, from any King, Prince, or foreign State.

Section. 10. No State shall enter into any Treaty, Alliance, or Confederation; grant Letters of Marque and Reprisal; coin Money; emit Bills of Credit; make any Thing but gold and silver Coin a Tender in Payment of Debts; pass any Bill of Attainder, ex post facto Law, or Law impairing the Obligation of Contracts, or grant any Title of Nobility.

No State shall, without the Consent of Congress, lay any Imposts or Duties on Imports or Exports, except what may be absolutely necessary for executing it's inspection Laws: and the net Produce of all Duties and Imposts, laid by any State on Imports or Exports, shall be for the Use of the Treasury of the United States; and all such Laws shall be subject to the Revision and Controul of Congress.

No State shall, without the Consent of Congress, lay any Duty of Tonnage, keep Troops, or Ships of War in time of Peace, enter into any Agreement or Compact with another State, or with a foreign Power, or engage in War, unless actually invaded, or in such imminent Danger as will not admit of delay.

Article. II.

Section. 1. The executive Power shall be vested in a President of the United States of America. He shall hold his Office during the Term of four Years, and, together with the Vice President, chosen for the same Term, be elected, as follows

Each State shall appoint, in such Manner as the Legislature thereof may direct, a Number of Electors, equal to the whole Number of Senators and Representatives to which the State may be entitled in the Congress: but no Senator or Representative, or Person holding an Office of Trust or Profit under the United States, shall be appointed an Elector.

The Electors shall meet in their respective States, and vote by Ballot for two Persons, of whom one at least shall not be an Inhabitant of the same State with themselves. And they shall make a List of all the Persons voted for, and of the Number of Votes for each; which List they shall sign and certify, and transmit sealed to the Seat of the Government of the United States, directed to the President of the Senate. The President of the Senate shall, in the Presence of the Senate and House of Representatives, open all the Certificates, and the Votes shall then be counted. The Person having the greatest Number of Votes shall be the President, if such Number be a Majority of the whole Number of Electors appointed; and if there be more than one who have such Majority, and have an equal Number of Votes, then the House of Representatives shall immediately chuse by Ballot one of them for President; and if no Person have a Majority, then from the five highest on the List the said House shall in like Manner chuse the President. But in chusing the President, the Votes shall be taken by States, the Representation from each State having one Vote; A quorum for this Purpose shall consist of a Member or Members from two thirds of the States, and a Majority of all the States shall be necessary to a Choice. In every Case, after the Choice of the President, the Person having the greatest Number of Votes of the Electors shall be the Vice President. But if there should remain two or more who have equal Votes, the Senate shall chuse from them by Ballot the Vice President.

The Congress may determine the Time of chusing the Electors, and the Day on which they shall give their Votes; which Day shall be the same throughout the United States.

No Person except a natural born Citizen, or a Citizen of the United States, at the time of the Adoption of this Constitution, shall be eligible to the Office of President; neither shall any Person be eligible to that Office who shall not have attained to the Age of thirty five Years, and been fourteen Years a Resident within the United States.

In Case of the Removal of the President from Office, or of his Death, Resignation, or Inability to discharge the Powers and Duties of the said Office, the Same shall devolve on the Vice President, and the Congress may by Law provide for the Case of Removal, Death, Resignation or Inability, both of the President and Vice President, declaring what Officer shall then act as President, and such Officer shall act accordingly, until the Disability be removed, or a President shall be elected.

The President shall, at stated Times, receive for his Services, a Compensation, which shall neither be encreased nor diminished during the Period for which he shall have been elected, and he shall not receive within that Period any other Emolument from the United States, or any of them.

Before he enter on the Execution of his Office, he shall take the following Oath or Affirmation:—"I do solemnly swear (or affirm) that I will faithfully execute the Office of President of the United States, and will to the best of my Ability, preserve, protect and defend the Constitution of the United States."

Section. 2. The President shall be Commander in Chief of the Army and Navy of the United States, and of the Militia of the several States, when called into the actual Service of the United States; he may require the Opinion, in writing, of the principal Officer in each of the executive Departments, upon any Subject relating to the Duties of their respective Offices, and he shall have Power to grant Reprieves and Pardons for Offences against the United States, except in Cases of Impeachment.

He shall have Power, by and with the Advice and Consent of the Senate, to make Treaties, provided two thirds of the Senators present concur; and he shall nominate, and by and with the Advice and Consent of the Senate, shall appoint Ambassadors, other public Ministers and Consuls, Judges of the supreme Court, and all other Officers of the United States, whose Appointments are not herein otherwise provided for, and which shall be established by Law: but the Congress may by Law vest the Appointment of such inferior Officers, as they think proper, in the President alone, in the Courts of Law, or in the Heads of Departments.

The President shall have Power to fill up all Vacancies that may happen during the Recess of the Senate, by granting Commissions which shall expire at the End of their next Session.

Section. 3. He shall from time to time give to the Congress Information of the State of the Union, and recommend to their Consideration such Measures as he shall judge necessary and expedient; he may, on extraordinary Occasions, convene both Houses, or either of them, and in Case of Disagreement between them, with Respect to the Time of Adjournment, he may adjourn them to such Time as he shall think proper; he shall receive Ambassadors and other public Ministers; he shall take Care that the Laws be faithfully executed, and shall Commission all the Officers of the United States.

Section. 4. The President, Vice President and all civil Officers of the United States, shall be removed from Office on Impeachment for, and Conviction of, Treason, Bribery, or other high Crimes and Misdemeanors.

Article III.

Section. 1. The judicial Power of the United States, shall be vested in one supreme Court, and in such inferior Courts as the Congress may from time to time ordain and establish. The Judges, both of the supreme and inferior Courts, shall hold their Offices during good Behaviour, and shall, at stated Times, receive for their Services, a Compensation, which shall not be diminished during their Continuance in Office.

Section. 2. The judicial Power shall extend to all Cases, in Law and Equity, arising under this Constitution, the Laws of the United States, and Treaties made, or which shall be made, under their Authority;—to all Cases affecting Ambassadors, other public Ministers and Consuls;—to all Cases of admiralty and maritime Jurisdiction;—to Controversies to which the United States shall be a Party;—to Controversies between two or more States;—between a State and Citizens of another State;—between Citizens of different States,—between Citizens of the same State claiming Lands under Grants of different States, and between a State, or the Citizens thereof, and foreign States, Citizens or Subjects.

In all Cases affecting Ambassadors, other public Ministers and Consuls, and those in which a State shall be Party, the supreme Court shall have original Jurisdiction. In all the other Cases before mentioned, the supreme Court shall have appellate Jurisdiction, both as to Law and Fact, with such Exceptions, and under such Regulations as the Congress shall make.

The Trial of all Crimes, except in Cases of Impeachment, shall be by Jury; and such Trial shall be held in the State where the said Crimes shall have been committed; but when not committed within any State, the Trial shall be at such Place or Places as the Congress may by Law have directed.

Section. 3. Treason against the United States, shall consist only in levying War against them, or in adhering to their Enemies, giving them Aid and Comfort. No Person shall be convicted of Treason unless on the Testimony of two Witnesses to the same overt Act, or on Confession in open Court.

The Congress shall have Power to declare the Punishment of Treason, but no Attainder of Treason shall work Corruption of Blood, or Forfeiture except during the Life of the Person attainted.

Article IV.

Section. 1. Full Faith and Credit shall be given in each State to the public Acts, Records, and judicial Proceedings of every other State. And the

Congress may by general Laws prescribe the Manner in which such Acts, Records and Proceedings shall be proved, and the Effect thereof.

Section. 2. The Citizens of each State shall be entitled to all Privileges and Immunities of Citizens in the several States.

A Person charged in any State with Treason, Felony, or other Crime, who shall flee from Justice, and be found in another State, shall on Demand of the executive Authority of the State from which he fled, be delivered up, to be removed to the State having Jurisdiction of the Crime.

No Person held to Service or Labour in one State, under the Laws thereof, escaping into another, shall, in Consequence of any Law or Regulation therein, be discharged from such Service or Labour, but shall be delivered up on Claim of the Party to whom such Service or Labour may be due.

Section. 3. New States may be admitted by the Congress into this Union; but no new State shall be formed or erected within the Jurisdiction of any other State; nor any State be formed by the Junction of two or more States, or Parts of States, without the Consent of the Legislatures of the States concerned as well as of the Congress.

The Congress shall have Power to dispose of and make all needful Rules and Regulations respecting the Territory or other Property belonging to the United States; and nothing in this Constitution shall be so construed as to Prejudice any Claims of the United States, or of any particular State.

Section. 4. The United States shall guarantee to every State in this Union a Republican Form of Government, and shall protect each of them against Invasion; and on Application of the Legislature, or of the Executive (when the Legislature cannot be convened) against domestic Violence.

Article. V.

The Congress, whenever two thirds of both Houses shall deem it necessary, shall propose Amendments to this Constitution, or, on the Application of the Legislatures of two thirds of the several States, shall call a Convention for proposing Amendments, which, in either Case, shall be valid to all Intents and Purposes, as Part of this Constitution, when ratified by the Legislatures of three fourths of the several States, or by Conventions in three fourths thereof, as the one or the other Mode of Ratification may be proposed by the Congress; Provided that no Amendment which may be made prior to the Year One thousand eight hundred and eight shall in any Manner affect the first and fourth Clauses in the Ninth Section of the first Article; and that no State, without its Consent, shall be deprived of its equal Suffrage in the Senate.

Article. VI.

All Debts contracted and Engagements entered into, before the Adoption of this Constitution, shall be as valid against the United States under this Constitution, as under the Confederation.

This Constitution, and the Laws of the United States which shall be made in Pursuance thereof; and all Treaties made, or which shall be made, under the Authority of the United States, shall be the supreme Law of the Land; and the Judges in every State shall be bound thereby, any Thing in the Constitution or Laws of any State to the Contrary notwithstanding.

The Senators and Representatives before mentioned, and the Members of the several State Legislatures, and all executive and judicial Officers, both of the United States and of the several States, shall be bound by Oath or Affirmation, to support this Constitution; but no religious Test shall ever be required as a Qualification to any Office or public Trust under the United States.

Article. VII.

The Ratification of the Conventions of nine States, shall be sufficient for the Establishment of this Constitution between the States so ratifying the Same.

The Word, "the," being interlined between the seventh and eighth Lines of the first Page, The Word "Thirty" being partly written on an Erazure in the fifteenth Line of the first Page, The Words "is tried" being interlined between the thirty second and thirty third Lines of the first Page and the Word "the" being interlined between the forty third and forty fourth Lines of the second Page.

Attest William Jackson Secretary

done in Convention by the Unanimous Consent of the States present the Seventeenth Day of September in the Year of our Lord one thousand seven hundred and Eighty seven and of the Independance of the United States of America the Twelfth In witness whereof We have hereunto subscribed our Names,

Go: Washington — Presidt. and deputy from Virginia

New Hampshire: John Langdon, Nicholas Gilman

Massachusetts: Nathaniel Gorham, Rufus King

Connecticut: Wm. Saml. Johnson, Roger Sherman

New York: Alexander Hamilton

New Jersey: Wil: Livingston, David Brearley, Wm. Paterson, Jona: Dayton

Pensylvania: B Franklin, Thomas Mifflin, Robt. Morris, Geo. Clymer, Thos. FitzSimons, Jared Ingersoll, James Wilson, Gouv Morris

Delaware: Geo: Read, Gunning Bedford jun, John Dickinson, Richard Bassett, Jaco: Broom

Maryland: James McHenry, Dan of St Thos. Jenifer, Danl. Carroll

Virginia: John Blair —, James Madison Jr.

North Carolina: Wm. Blount, Richd. Dobbs Spaight, Hu Williamson

South Carolina: J. Rutledge, Charles Cotesworth Pinckney, Charles Pinckney, Pierce Butler

Georgia: William Few, Abr Baldwin

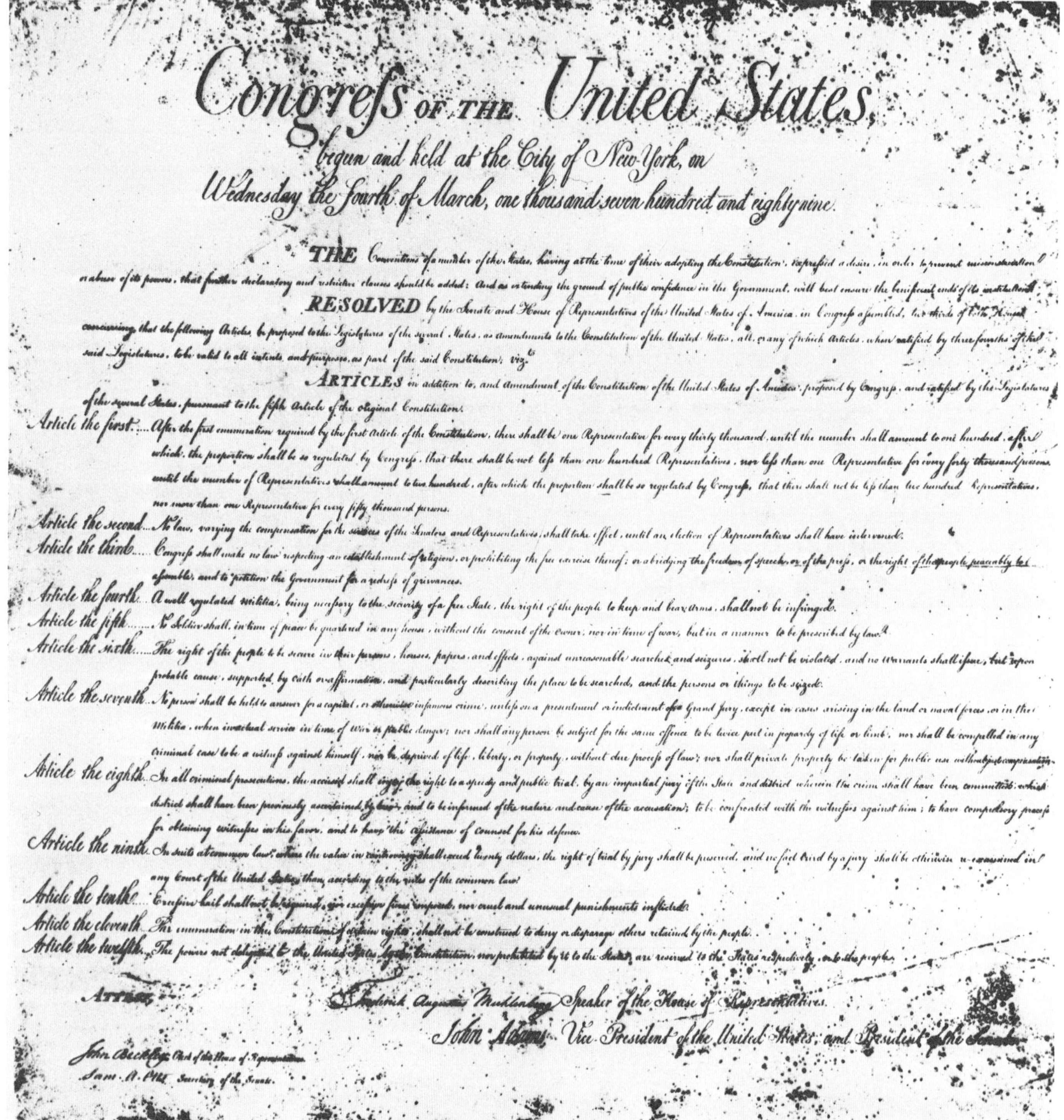

Congress of the United States,
begun and held at the City of New-York, on
Wednesday the Fourth of March, one thousand seven hundred and eighty nine.

THE Conventions of a number of the States, having at the time of their adopting the Constitution, expressed a desire, in order to prevent misconstruction or abuse of its powers, that further declaratory and restrictive clauses should be added: And as extending the ground of public confidence in the Government, will best ensure the beneficent ends of its institution.

RESOLVED by the Senate and House of Representatives of the United States of America, in Congress assembled, two thirds of both Houses concurring, that the following Articles be proposed to the Legislatures of the several States, as amendments to the Constitution of the United States, all, or any of which Articles, when ratified by three fourths of the said Legislatures, to be valid to all intents and purposes, as part of the said Constitution; viz.

ARTICLES in addition to, and Amendment of the Constitution of the United States of America, proposed by Congress, and ratified by the Legislatures of the several States, pursuant to the fifth Article of the original Constitution.

Article the first.... After the first enumeration required by the first Article of the Constitution, there shall be one Representative for every thirty thousand, until the number shall amount to one hundred, after which, the proportion shall be so regulated by Congress, that there shall be not less than one hundred Representatives, nor less than one Representative for every forty thousand persons, until the number of Representatives shall amount to two hundred, after which the proportion shall be so regulated by Congress, that there shall not be less than two hundred Representatives, nor more than one Representative for every fifty thousand persons.

Article the second.... No law, varying the compensation for the services of the Senators and Representatives, shall take effect, until an election of Representatives shall have intervened.

Article the third.... Congress shall make no law respecting an establishment of religion, or prohibiting the free exercise thereof; or abridging the freedom of speech, or of the press, or the right of the people peaceably to assemble, and to petition the Government for a redress of grievances.

Article the fourth.... A well regulated militia, being necessary to the security of a free State, the right of the people to keep and bear Arms, shall not be infringed.

Article the fifth.... No Soldier shall, in time of peace be quartered in any house, without the consent of the Owner, nor in time of war, but in a manner to be prescribed by law.

Article the sixth.... The right of the people to be secure in their persons, houses, papers, and effects, against unreasonable searches and seizures, shall not be violated, and no Warrants shall issue, but upon probable cause, supported by oath or affirmation, and particularly describing the place to be searched, and the persons or things to be seized.

Article the seventh.... No person shall be held to answer for a capital, or otherwise infamous crime, unless on a presentment or indictment of a Grand Jury, except in cases arising in the land or naval forces, or in the Militia, when in actual service in time of War or public danger; nor shall any person be subject for the same offence to be twice put in jeopardy of life or limb; nor shall be compelled in any criminal case, to be a witness against himself, nor be deprived of life, liberty, or property, without due process of law; nor shall private property be taken for public use without just compensation.

Article the eighth.... In all criminal prosecutions, the accused shall enjoy the right to a speedy and public trial, by an impartial jury of the State and district wherein the crime shall have been committed, which district shall have been previously ascertained by law, and to be informed of the nature and cause of the accusation; to be confronted with the witnesses against him; to have compulsory process for obtaining witnesses in his favor, and to have the assistance of counsel for his defence.

Article the ninth.... In suits at common law, where the value in controversy shall exceed twenty dollars, the right of trial by jury shall be preserved, and no fact tried by a jury shall be otherwise re-examined in any Court of the United States, than according to the rules of the common law.

Article the tenth.... Excessive bail shall not be required, nor excessive fines imposed, nor cruel and unusual punishments inflicted.

Article the eleventh.... The enumeration in the Constitution, of certain rights, shall not be construed to deny or disparage others retained by the people.

Article the twelfth.... The powers not delegated to the United States by the Constitution, nor prohibited by it to the States, are reserved to the States respectively, or to the people.

Frederick Augustus Muhlenberg Speaker of the House of Representatives.
John Adams, Vice-President of the United States, and President of the Senate.

ATTEST,
John Beckley, Clerk of the House of Representatives.
Sam. A. Otis Secretary of the Senate.

THE JOINT RESOLUTION PROPOSING A BILL OF RIGHTS